SMOOTH RIDING
THE PRIDMORE WAY

SMOOTH RIDING

THE PRIDMORE WAY

Advanced Motorcycle Skills through CONFIDENCE and CONTROL

REG PRIDMORE
with Geoff Drake

Whitehorse Press
Center Conway, New Hampshire

Front and back cover photos by Ian Donald.
Title page photo courtesy Suzuki Motor Corporation.
Photo this page by Ian Donald.

Illustrations by Joe Kerr.
Cover and book design by Jessica Armstrong.

SPECIAL NOTICE: The information in this book is true and complete to the best of our knowledge. All recommendations are made without any guarantee on the part of the author or Publisher, who disclaim any liability incurred in connection with the use of the techniques and concepts described in this book. Always wear protective gear and observe the speed limit!

The name Whitehorse Press is a trademark of Kennedy Associates.

Whitehorse Press books are also available at discounts in bulk quantity for sales and promotional use. For details about special sales or for a catalog of motorcycling books and videos, write to the publisher:

Whitehorse Press
107 East Conway Road,
Center Conway, NH 03813
Phone: 603-356-6556 or 800-531-1133
Email: Orders@WhitehorsePress.com
Internet: www.WhitehorsePress.com

CONTENTS

ACKNOWLEDGMENTS

After spending almost 50 years as a motorcyclist, it's great to be able to give credit to all of those who made my adventure thus far such a rush. I guess Mum and Dad head the list of thanks for giving me the nod to get my first motorcycle. They agreed even though my cousin almost lost the works at a young age on one of those dangerous contraptions!

People like Les Wright who trusted me to wick his Triumph Tiger 100 off into the distance for the very first time. That was the clincher back in 1955. Cheers to all my street racing teen mates: Kenny Jones, Brian, Pete, Dave Fox, and Dick Butt who all challenged me to ride faster than was safe, thus eventually forcing me to take it to the track.

Cheers to Greeves importer Nick Nicholson for loaning me the 250cc racer once I came to the U.S. And in the late '60s to my good friends and former bosses Pat Petticord and Chief Galbraith who became stepping-stones to my club-racing career.

Professionalism stepped in around '71 (that's when you get cash to do this dirty job) and Brian Slark of Norton Villiers and George Wenn were great assets in my early Commando days. Thanks Brian and George. People like those who ran Bell Helmets, Bates Leathers, and Dunlop Tire and so many others who had great faith in my ability to carry their banners. Butler & Smith BMW,

Dr. Peter Adams, Helmut Kern, Matt Capri, Udo Gietl, and of course the mighty Todd Schuster made most of the '70s flash by. Then Racecrafters and Craig Vetter carried the big Kawasaki banner from '77 to '79. Extra thanks goes to my No. 1 wrench, Pierre Des Roches, who sadly lost his life in a military helicopter crash in the mid '90s. Thanks also to my hero and friend, the late Don Vesco, who sponsored my Yamaha TZ750 sidecar efforts in the Isle of Man, along with building wiz Rob North. Thanks Kenny Greene for being the greatest passenger.

But the current efforts wouldn't be possible without Honda. These past 10 years with Honda and Honda Rider's Club of America have been some of the most fun of all. Special thanks to Honda's Ray Blank and Charlie Keller and of course Mr. Honda's superb line of modern-day hardware, which makes today's motorcycling more exciting than ever.

Many thanks to all of the gracious sponsors including Shoei helmets, Erion Racing, Helimot, Zero Gravity, Dynojet Research, DP Brakes, and of course, it's still Dunlop Tire keeping me on the edge. And I can't forget all my great instructor friends and their helpers. You have helped make CLASS what it is today, having helped thousands of motorcyclists become better and safer riders. Thanks Gigi for all your effort put forth over the years. Lastly, this book would not have been possible without writer Geoff Drake. Your hard work, research, and many late night phone calls kept us on track when I was buried deep in school dates and traveling.

I hope you enjoy the reading you're about to embark upon, and I hope to see you at the track or on the road sometime soon. Until then, ride safe and think fast!

Cheers!

Reg Pridmore

(Below, Ian Donald Photography)
(Top photo courtesy EuroTech)

FOREWORD BY KEVIN ERION

In the '80s my brother Craig and I attended CLASS at Riverside Raceway. I can honestly say it was a turning point in my life and career. Though I'd ridden since I was 15, motorcycles were just a form of transportation for me up until that point.

I was so filled with excitement and adrenaline that day. But my enduring memory is how Reggie brought a sense of calm to that tornado of emotions. He made me realize that I could get something out of that experience besides the immediate thrill of being on the track. I was possessed by the idea of being a better rider. By the end of the day, I knew that I had to come back.

The rest, as they say, is history. I took a second CLASS, and a third, and a fourth—and never stopped. I went from being a novice who used the motorcycle for transportation, to being a CLASS instructor, and embarking on a racing career, and then to owning a team and a successful parts business. I've been a CLASS guest instructor now for 10 years.

That day at Riverside Raceway opened a door for me. I didn't even know the door was there, much less what was on the other side. Reggie started that process of exploration.

Ultimately, what Reggie teaches can save your life. He provides a tool: it's called control. The level of control that can be achieved through his techniques is almost inconceivable to the average rider. It's not necessarily about going fast. It's about experiencing the motorcycle in a new way, and applying it to real world riding.

Reggie also makes things fun. He genuinely wants people to be better riders, and you can tell he enjoys the process. It's evident in his big smile, and in his British humor. It's evident in this book. Teaching is not just a routine for Reggie—you get the impression that he is having as much fun as the students.

I think Reggie would be the first one to tell you that you can't learn everything from a book like the one you're holding now. But what it can do is provide a foundation for the lifelong learning process you are about to undertake. I hope you let this book start that process for you—just as Reggie's teaching started my own transformation that day at Riverside Raceway.

Kevin Erion

Kevin Erion is the founder of Erion Racing, the leading manufacturer and supplier of aftermarket components for Honda motorcycles. Erion won two AMA Pro Twins championships in the late 1980s, and the team he created has forged one of the most stellar records in AMA road racing. Erion bikes and riders have won six out of eight titles in the AMA's big-bore road racing class on Honda's CBR900RR and CBR929RR, and two 600 SuperSport championships with Honda's best-selling CBR600.

(Photos courtesy American Honda Motor Co., Inc.)

INTRODUCTION

THE BEST OF TIMES

This is a great time to ride a motorcycle. Today there are so many excellent bikes to choose from. We're fortunate to be riding in an era when the bike takes some of the hard work out of riding well. Most modern motorcycles accelerate, stop, and handle extremely well. Maybe too well. While all these advances can help you be a better, safer rider, the motorcycle is not foolproof. Today's bikes, for all their advances, can spit you off before you even know there's a problem. (Kevin Wing Photography)

ALTHOUGH MY BACKGROUND IS RACING, THIS BOOK SERVES EVERY TYPE OF RIDER, ON ANY TYPE OF BIKE. *My method of teaching came from racing, where control is everything. That's one of the centerpieces of my riding philosophy, along with an emphasis on smoothness and focus. Throughout my career, I've noticed that the thinking riders are the ones that win. That's as true today as it's ever been, and it's what I try to impart in CLASS. (Ian Donald Photography)*

How do you harness the motorcycle's capability and use it to your advantage? You have to know how to "talk" to it. Communication implies an exchange: You give input, and you receive feedback. And to have this exchange, you have to know the language. It's called "control."

Control is the core of my riding philosophy. It starts with the proper attitude, including such things as discipline and focus. In this book I devote an entire chapter to attitude and mental awareness. With this foundation in place, you add the proper technique to make the rider and machine flow as one. I include many chapters focused on concrete skills such as throttle management, braking, proper lines, and rpm range. Control represents the sum of all these factors, used in exactly the right measure, and at the right time.

A philosophy of control is valid both on the track and on the street. Control is the essence of being fast, and it is the essence of being safe, wherever you ride.

LIFELONG LEARNING

I've been riding and racing for almost 50 years. Even though I feel I have a very good sense of control, I continue to search for more *every time I throw a leg over the bike.* I know I'm only human. My goal is to keep on having a good time on my motorcycle, and keep myself alive. This means I need to constantly re-examine every aspect of what I do. I never take anything for granted. Neither should you.

I'm always taken aback by riders who have 10, 20, or more years of experience, and didn't think they could learn anything by coming to CLASS. Afterward, these riders consistently tell me how excited they are to learn new techniques and become faster and smoother. Many of them write me about the great success they've had putting my suggestions to work. Already, you've shown a willingness to learn, just by picking up this book. That's a good sign.

WHO IS THIS BOOK FOR?

You might think that since my background is racing, that what I teach is only for racers. Or conversely, maybe you've heard that CLASS is just for street riders. Actually, neither is accurate.

What I teach is for anyone seeking to be better at the task at hand: riding the motorcycle. When you learn how to ride properly—*and how to be in control*—you can take your skills anywhere. Here are just a few types of riders who can expect to benefit from this book:

Beginners. The techniques I teach are for riders of all experience levels. They are particularly helpful to new riders who want to develop good riding habits early. This not only helps you ride well right now, but also means you don't have to break bad habits down the road.

Street riders. I ride on the street regularly and it's a lot of fun. But I also know there are people out there who are waiting to get me. Some of you may be out to get yourselves; you just don't know it yet! I'll teach you skills that will help keep you safe—from yourself, and from others.

Experienced riders. My techniques can help experienced riders elevate their skills a notch or two. This book can also help you correct bad habits you may have acquired. I'll teach you the control required to be a safer, more confident rider.

Track riders. Perhaps you've been street riding for a number of years, and you don't need any help in this department—you just want to be faster on the track. This book can help you accomplish that.

WHAT WILL YOU LEARN?

This book will delve into all aspects of riding: from mental techniques, to concrete skills, to technical topics that will help you enjoy your bike to its fullest capability. There are chapters devoted to riding psychology, throttle management, cornering, shifting, body positioning, and

SIMPLE, BUT EFFECTIVE.
CLASS instructors such as Ted Holman teach simple but effective techniques—the same ones you'll learn in this book. It's up to you to make them part of the way you do business on the motorcycle. (Ian Donald Photography)

braking. You'll also find tips on bike setup and plenty of information on traffic techniques and accident avoidance. Throughout, I'll illustrate points with anecdotes from my own riding, racing, and teaching career.

OK, you're probably wondering: "What makes this book different from other motorcycling skills books, and why should I read it?" I can confidently say that a lot of what I teach you won't find in any other book or riding school.

Racing made me take a good look at my skills. Most of my techniques were honed at the racetrack. For instance, I put a lot of emphasis on smoothness. I believe that being smooth isn't just an artful or elegant way to ride the bike (though it is those things, too). You need to be smooth before you can go fast, and you need to be smooth to be safe. I also put a lot of emphasis on "body steering": using subtle weight shifts to initiate turns, rather than being forceful with the handlebar. You won't read a lot about these topics in the typical motorcycling curriculum. But I promise you, *these techniques work.*

I also have a unique approach to braking. If I can boast a little, braking is something that I do very well. This skill is extremely important to the racer, but just as important to the street rider. You need to know how to handle your emotions and use your brakes properly.

One of the most common reasons riders crash on the street is panic combined with improper braking techniques (usually overemphasizing the rear brake). I also recommend using two fingers on your front brake instead of four, to give you control of the throttle with the rest of your hand. There is a lot of misinformation out there when it comes to braking!

Most of the techniques you'll learn are simple but effective. It's up to you to make them part of your way of doing business on the motorcycle. If you open your mind and study what I offer, these methods can benefit you. But I won't wag my finger at you and say you "must" do this or you "must" do that. I ask only that you try what I suggest and see if it works for you.

WILLING TO LEARN.
CLASS riders consistently tell me how excited they are to learn new techniques and become faster and smoother. By coming to CLASS, they have shown a willingness to learn—a critical step. By picking up this book, you've shown the same openness to learning. That's great! (Ian Donald Photography)

I've helped thousands of CLASS students over the years, and I'd like to help you, too. It's a great time to be riding. Do it well and stay alive!

WHO IS THIS GUY, REG PRIDMORE?

Before you accept what I have to say about riding a motorcycle, you deserve to know a little bit about me.

I was born in London, and some of my earliest memories are of World War II. It was a hard time—we were literally bombed out of our house. We relocated outside the city in Hornchurch, Essex. There was an airfield there, a Spitfire base, and I quickly developed a fascination for airplanes. Even today, I'm still crazy about planes. (I own two planes—a Citabria and a Globe Swift—and enjoy acrobatic flying.) Looking back, maybe it was the beginning of something—a need for speed.

At the time I had a cousin who rode motorcycles. He wasn't exactly well regarded in the family for this, but of course his involvement in bikes fascinated me. When I was 15, a friend lent me his bike for a ride down the street. Well, I took it a little further than around the block. Being on a motorcycle was instantly a great feeling: something I remember to this day. You only get a feeling like that maybe once or twice in your life. The seed was planted. I had to have a bike.

My parents weren't too keen on the idea, because by then my cousin had been involved in a bad accident. But I continued my plea. I told my Dad, "It's so great; you can see all around. Riding is the best feeling!" Eventually he caved in. I sold everything I could put my hands on to buy a used 1951 350cc Triumph 3T. That was in '55. I

LEFT. *In 1955 I obtained my first bike—a used 1951 350cc Triumph 3T. I'd hang out with a dozen other teenagers and we'd go to the cafe and talk motorcycles until we were sick. It was a great time in my life! (Photo courtesy Reg Pridmore)*

RIGHT. *In the 1990s—more than 10 years after my last race—a unique opportunity came my way: to compete in the company of some of the world's best racers from the '50s, '60s, '70s, and '80s in the Battle of the Legends. Here I lead coming out of the Turn 5 Horseshoe at Daytona in 1996. Hot in pursuit are Jay Springsteen, Gary Nixon, and Yvon Duhamel. (Photo courtesy Don Bok)*

picked up my new bike and my first ride was in the pouring rain. Of course I didn't have a helmet or proper clothes yet. I even managed to get a ticket. When I got home, looking like a drowned rat, my Dad took one look at me and said, "Isn't it great? You can see all around. A great feeling, eh?" It didn't matter. I was hooked.

That little bike became my sole transportation. Snow, sleet, freezing rain, it didn't matter; I was out there. I'd hang out with a dozen other teenagers and we'd go to the cafe and talk motorcycles until we were sick. It was probably some of the best times in my life.

I've always tried to use my head when it comes to motorcycling and be a thinking rider. But I also had some pretty close ones on the street. I'd moved up to bigger, faster bikes and it got to the point where I was scaring myself. I knew if I kept riding that way I was going to get

1955

- First motorcycle, 1951 350cc Triumph 3T.
- Early motorcycling experiences: cafe racing in England, hanging out at the famous ACE Cafe, Ted's Diner, and Ma Johnson's. The start of a lifelong obsession with the sport, and the basis for many fond memories.

1959

- First race win! Reg enters one of his first races at Silverstone, England, and wins in the blinding rain riding a Triumph 500cc Tiger 100C.

1960–1961

- Travels to tracks outside of London competing in Autocycle Union (ACU) races on Triumph Tiger 100C and AJS 7R 350.

1964

- Emigrates to America, settling in Santa Barbara, California.
- Meets Nick Nicholson, who gets him involved in club racing. Travels to events throughout California, sometimes competing in six or seven races per day.

1965

- Suffers huge racing crash, resulting in compound fractures of both bones in his lower right leg and fracturing his skull. Out of competition for a year.

1966

- Begins racing sidecars as a means to get back into racing after the crash. (Walking and riding solo were both difficult during this recuperation period.)

1968

- Wins American Federation of Motorcyclists (AFM) championship riding 1958 500cc Norton Manx.
- Wins sidecar championship on 650cc Triumph-powered outfit with passenger Ernie Caesar.

1971

- Partial Norton sponsorship at the club level. Competes in his first American Motorcyclist Association (AMA) race at Daytona, Florida, with good friend George Kerker of Kerker Exhaust fame, both on Commando 750s.

- Begins long and productive sponsorship arrangement with BMW importer Butler & Smith, racing air-cooled BMW R75/5.
- Opens BMW Dealership, RPM Cycles (Reg Pridmore Motorcycles), in Santa Barbara.
- Races Norton Commando 750-powered sidecar at Isle of Man with Ernie Caesar.

1972–1973

- Competes in American Federation of Motorcyclists (AFM) racing on BMWs with an occasional AMA National. BMW backs this effort in order to improve its image and promote a new line of bikes. Although the bikes aren't fully competitive, Reg successfully campaigns them on the club race circuit.

1974

- Begins racing and winning on Butler & Smith BMW R90S, tuned to produce more than 90 horsepower.
- Wins his first AMA National race at Ontario Motor Speedway, California.
- Teaches first riding class at Denver Fairgrounds. Conducts occasional classes during the next few years in the midst of a busy racing career.

In the early '70s Butler & Smith offered me a ride on a BMW twin. Those years with BMW were great—I was beating the big Japanese teams on what most people considered a touring bike. (Photo courtesy Matt Capri)

1976

- Wins the inaugural AMA Superbike championship: the first of three. Last year of fruitful association with Butler & Smith. This includes a second place at Daytona in a photo finish alongside teammate Steve McLaughlin, as well as wins at Riverside and Laguna Seca, California.
- Returns to Isle of Man sidecar racing with passenger Kenny Greene on a Don Vesco sponsored/Rob North built Yamaha TZ750-powered sidecar.

1977

- Begins Racecrafters sponsorship, riding Kawasaki KZ1000 that produces 140-plus horsepower.
- Wins second AMA Superbike championship with very consistent podiums but only one race win, at Pocono, Pennsylvania.
- Returns to Isle of Man for more sidecar racing with Kenny Greene and the Vesco/North Yamaha TZ750. Laps the 37-plus mile road course at an average speed of 101.46 mph.

1978

- Competes at Isle of Man with Greene on the Vesco/North Yamaha TZ750 sidecar.
- Crash at Suzuka, Japan, lands Reg in a body cast with a broken shoulder. Misses Loudon, New Hampshire, national but convinces the doctor to staple him together for the final at Laguna Seca. A fourth place finish is all that's needed for the Superbike championship and Reg makes it happen.
- Wins third AMA Superbike championship on Craig Vetter-sponsored Kawasaki.

1979

- Competes at Isle of Man with Greene on the Vesco/North Yamaha TZ750 sidecar.

I won the championship for Kawasaki in '77 and '78, sponsored by fairing-maker Craig Vetter. This photo is from Bathhurst, Australia in '79—my last year of racing. (Photo courtesy Paul Kirkman)

- A mechanical DNF at Daytona is just the beginning of a difficult year that ends with a massive crash at Laguna Seca, in which another rider takes out Reg. It results in a broken hip, wrist, and ankle, and leads to eventual retirement from racing.

1981–1982

- Conceives and implements classes for better street riding technique. Maintains full-time teaching agenda in addition to running RPM BMW Franchise. BMW North America sponsors the school and original program begins.

1986

- Formally begins CLASS (California's Leading Advanced Safety School).

1992

- Re-enters racing to compete in special series, sponsored by the American Historic Racing Motorcycle Association and BMW of North America, called the Battle of the Legends

1993

- Sells RPM Cycles; now CLASS is sole focus.

1996

- CLASS grows to more than 50 sessions per year, visiting the nation's best tracks.

2002

- Inducted into the AMA Hall of Fame.

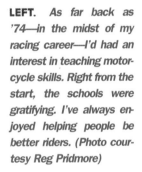

hurt. I needed a place to develop my skills. So in the late '50s, I decided to get off the road and onto the track.

MY FIRST RACES

A friend and I had three bikes by then: a 500cc Triumph Tiger 100C that I had developed into a competent race bike, an AJS 7R 350, and a little 125. It was hard to get an entry into the races back then, so we would enter all three bikes in the hope that the racing body, the Autocycle Union, would accept one. We went to the tracks, sleeping in the back of a van and "doing a Dick Mann" (a legendary racer known for his single-minded dedication to the sport). I can even remember sleeping in our leathers to keep warm. We were so poor we couldn't afford to stay in hotels or B & Bs.

The first race I ever won was at the famous Silverstone course. During that year I raced all over England at tracks like Brands Hatch, Snetterton, Aintree, Aberdare Park, and Mallory Park. That was in '60. I really only raced that one year in England, because other commitments intervened: I did a stint in the army, got married, and sold all my bikes to buy a house.

Meanwhile, I'd always had a strong attraction to the U.S. and wanted to go to California some day. In '64, my wife and I decided to sell it all and emigrate. We packed everything in my beautiful Studebaker Hawk and boarded the SS United States, bound for America. We arrived in New York, and drove across the country to California, taking in the sights along the way, including the Grand Canyon and Disneyland.

LIFE IN AMERICA

On the ship across the Atlantic someone told me: Don't settle in Los Angeles. Go 100 miles up the coast to Santa Barbara; it's much nicer. I took this advice, and have lived in Santa Barbara and the surrounding area for 40 years now.

I really had no intention of getting back into motorcycle racing when I came to the U.S. I was more into cars at that point. In fact, my first job in Santa Barbara was pumping gas at a Texaco station. However, in England I'd worked in the motorcycle industry, schooling in Coventry (with Triumph) and working on Triumphs, BSAs, Nortons, and also for the Greeves factory. I was able to parley that experience into a job at Honda of Santa Barbara.

It was there that I met Nick Nicholson, owner of Nick Nicholson Motors, which sold Greeves motorcycles in North Hollywood. He loaned me a bike and got me into club racing. I'd go to Vacaville, or Riverside, or other small tracks. I was getting tons of track time, and really enjoying it. Before long, I was elected president of the AFM (American Federation of Motorcyclists). This California club had a huge membership then, and I raced with the AFM until I turned pro in '71.

I was really starting to devote myself to the sport. I would go to a club event and race six or seven classes in a day. I'd jump off one machine that shifted up one and down three on the left, and then immediately hop on another that shifted down one and up four on the right. It was crazy, but I loved it.

Unfortunately I had a terrible accident in '65, suffering a double compound leg fracture and a skull fracture, among other things. I also bled from my ear, which I know now was not a good thing. It was a horrible crash, but it had a silver lining: among other things it led me to racing sidecars. That was my transition back to racing after the crash. My passenger was Ernie Caesar, and before long we were traveling everywhere on the race circuit. Sidecar racing first instilled the value of being smooth. With a sidecar, I found that any jerky motions have a terrible effect on your passenger. As Ernie made his transitions back and forth in the chair, I had to be super smooth to avoid having him miss his handholds and throwing him out of the sidecar.

When my leg had almost completely healed, I got back on a solo bike. I found that the value of smoothness was apparent: the effect wasn't limited to sidecars. From that point, I started to emphasize smoothness in all my riding. And it proved successful. In '68 I won the AFM 500cc championship on a 1958 Norton Manx. I also won the sidecar category on a Triumph powered machine. My racing career was really starting to come together.

PRO RACING

In '71 I went to Daytona for the first time on a Norton Commando. Later that year BMW importer Butler & Smith offered me a ride on a BMW twin. It was a relationship I'd maintain until 1976, but at the time I didn't know what to expect. I'd been racing for fun, but now, racing against the likes of Grand National dirt track champion David Aldana, it seemed like it was time to start developing some professionalism—and I was getting paid to do so.

Those years with BMW were great: I was beating the big Japanese teams on what most people considered a "touring bike" (an air-cooled, horizontal twin with a drive shaft). It

made each win much more satisfying. My last full year with BMW was '76, when I placed second at Daytona in a photo finish alongside teammate Steve McLaughlin. But the year proceeded to get better and I won the American Motorcyclist Association (AMA) Superbike championship for the first time. The very next year, after a miserable Daytona, BMW stopped competing on the road racing circuit.

Almost immediately Racecrafters offered me a ride on a Kawasaki KZ1000. Racecrafters was a well-known mail order motorcycle parts company of the day. A great team was put together which included my new tuner, Pierre Des Roches. Pierre and I would go on to have a longtime race relationship as well as a good friendship.

Those Kawasakis were tough birds to ride: they didn't handle. We called them "flexi-flyers." Even though the handling was evil, the motor was strong. Pierre would always make it go a little better, and eventually we were getting 141 horsepower on the dynamometer. He got a lot out of that bike, and we had some good times together. I won the championship for Kawasaki in '77. In '78 and '79 I was sponsored by fairing maker Craig Vetter.

Nowadays people look back at what we racers achieved in the '70s and they think it was easy. But it wasn't. True, the machinery today is a vast

CLASS BEGINNINGS.
This is one of my early schools at Riverside Raceway, California. I immediately became motivated by the idea of helping students master the arts of control and finesse. (Photo courtesy Reg Pridmore)

step forward, but the drive and competitive spirit was every bit as strong back then.

Riding those old bikes also helped solidify my belief in the value of being smooth. The BMWs and Kawasakis I rode were basically street bikes. They had very little ground clearance and they were very twitchy. As we got additional power out of the bikes, they became even more violent to ride. They didn't have the tremendously stiff perimeter or trellis frames of today's machines.

The Kawasaki was producing more than 140 horsepower, but it wasn't designed to handle more than 100! Consequently, it was crucial to monitor all my inputs: throttle, braking, and body movements. That was something that really paid off for me. I emphasized smoothness my whole career, and it forms the basis of my instructional technique today.

LIFE AFTER RACING

In '79 during practice at Laguna Seca, a young rider (who in my opinion shouldn't have been on the track) fixated on me as I went around him in a turn. He couldn't make the turn and slammed into the back of my bike driving me into the Armco barrier. I hit the barrier hard and broke my hip, wrist, and ankle. I was out of contention for a

year. At the same time, the motorcycle industry was in a bit of a lull and sponsorship was getting scarce. I never raced professionally again.

During the early '70s, I'd started RPM: Reg Pridmore Motorcycles, a BMW franchise in Santa Barbara. It was doing well, and without the racing to keep me out of town I was able to focus more heavily on that. The dealership kept me very busy and in late '79 I moved the shop 30 miles south to Ventura. But I still felt the track held more for me.

As far back as '74, in the midst of my racing career, I'd had an interest in teaching motorcycling skills. I conducted an informal class at the Denver Fairgrounds in '74 with about 40 people. I just laid out some cones and did it. Then I followed up with schools in Riverside and Ontario, California. Right from the start, the schools were gratifying. Even though I did them infrequently, I got a lot of interest. I also realized that it was something I genuinely liked to do. I've always enjoyed helping people become riders and felt like it was something I could do to give back to the sport I enjoyed so much.

There was another, more sobering reason I was drawn to teaching. As early as '70—the dawn of the Japanese four-cylinder superbike—I began to see so many young kids going out and killing themselves on Honda CB750s and Kawasaki Z1 900s. I once even tried contacting the state in an effort to raise funding for education. I gathered statistics on the number of kids 18 and younger who were dying on overpowered bikes. But the state didn't want to hear about it. I just hated to see this carnage, plus it was giving motorcycling a bad name. I thought, maybe there is something I can do. The fact that I'd been a successful racer helped bring attention to my cause.

Before long, I realized it wasn't just the young kids that needed to learn control and improve their skills. I became motivated by the idea of helping anyone, at any age, be a better rider.

CLASS IS BORN

That was the genesis of CLASS: California's Leading Advanced Safety School. It actually began in '82 under a different name. In 1986 I incorporated and CLASS became a nationwide series backed by BMW. In 1995 a strong bond

AT THE TRACK THESE DAYS I RIDE A CAMERA BIKE. *Small lenses protrude from the front and back, allowing me to film students and review the videos in the classroom. Its a great instructional tool. (Photo courtesy EuroTech)*

was made with Honda and they became my primary sponsor. Beyond Honda there are several other distinguished companies that sponsor CLASS, including Dunlop, Erion Racing, Shoei, Helimot, DP-Brakes, Zero Gravity, and Dynojet Research. All of these companies have helped me make CLASS what it is today: the best street riding school in the USA.

Pretty quickly, the schools went from six or eight per year, to a couple of dozen and more. I had a full life: with CLASS, my motorcycle franchise, and raising my son, Jason. I had a lot going on. But it was an enjoyable way to make a living because I was doing what I loved best, motorcycling.

I've always enjoyed the life and the camaraderie I have with my instructors, some of whom have been with me for a long time. But most of all, I like seeing people leave with big smiles on their faces. People come up to me after class and say, "You

know what? That really works. And it's made me safer for the street." It's extremely gratifying.

I also get a lot of satisfaction from instilling an attitude of lifelong learning in my students. You can always be a better rider. Some of my students come back time and time again. They can never get enough training. That's the attitude I like to see. Whether it means coming to CLASS, or just treating every day on the motorcycle as a learning experience.

My method of teaching came from racing, where control is everything. That's one of the centerpieces of my riding philosophy, along with an emphasis on smoothness and focus. Throughout my career, I've noticed that the thinking riders are the ones that win. That's as true today as it's ever been. That's what I try to impart in CLASS. It's also the basis for this book. Enjoy, and ride smart!

CLASS BEGINS WITH AN INTRODUCTION TO THE TRACK. *We visit each corner, discussing the correct line, braking points, and the like. Here we are at Laguna Seca Raceway. People can't wait to get going, but I want them to think carefully about what they will be doing out there! (Ian Donald Photography)*

ATTITUDE

IT STARTS IN YOUR HEAD

I think of myself as a friendly, personable chap. After all, motorcycling is fun, and that's why most of us ride. People come to CLASS not just to learn, but also to enjoy themselves. The feeling of smoothly piloting a bike around the track at race speeds—without the intrusion of speed limits—is truly wonderful.

(Photo courtesy Suzuki Motor Corporation)

However, over the years I've developed a sense of urgency and concern for my students. More and more, I challenge them in the classroom. This doesn't mean I get verbally offensive. But when I see they've gained confidence, I try to wake them up. Because with confidence comes complacency. And there is no place for complacency in motorcycling.

The fact that you're reading this book tells me that you have some idea of the risks of motorcycling and the level of care and focus that's required. You're making an effort to improve your skills, and that's great. You also know that on the track, simple mistakes can hurt you badly. On the road, they can get you killed.

Much of this book will focus on the concrete skills of motorcycling. For example, throttle management, braking, proper lines, and rpm range. But all these things rest on a foundation of attitude. Without proper attitude, you won't be able to utilize these concrete skills and become a better, faster, safer rider.

LESSONS LEARNED

I made my career in racing, but I came from a street background. I rode the streets in England pretty hard, and I learned quite a bit along the way. I actually got off the roads for a while in my teens because I sensed I was putting myself in danger. It seemed like I was heading for "the big one." I knew I would be better off at the track, where I could work on my skills without the variables of traffic, bad roads, and other environmental hazards.

My son Jason did the reverse; he started out on the track and learned a lot prior to riding on the street. When he finally did ride on the roads, he was very aware of the hazards. Track riding gave him a deep sense of where he had to be to avoid danger. It also taught him restraint. He learned a lot of lessons in the track environment.

You don't need to ride on the track to be a good street rider (though I guarantee it will help you). But wherever you ride, you need to be acutely aware of your limits. And you need to treat every

FOR MANY RIDERS, RIDING ON THE TRACK IS LIKE BEING SET LOOSE IN A CANDY STORE. *It's also a great laboratory in which to hone their skills. But at the same time, they must temper their exuberance with discipline! (Ian Donald Photography)*

ride as a learning opportunity. I found out a lot of these things the hard way. I'm offering you the benefit of my nearly 50 years experience so that maybe you won't make the same mistakes.

CONTROL: IT'S ALL IN YOUR RIGHT HAND

If people attending CLASS learn one thing, it should be this: control. That's the big one for me. It's so important that I put it right in everyone's face, on a big white board in the front of the classroom: C-O-N-T-R-O-L. It's what we all should be searching for as motorcyclists.

I think we all have a bit of Jekyll and Hyde in us when we're riding. We need to recognize that there are those two persons within ourselves. There is the person that always wants to go faster, and the other person who is reasonable and safe.

There's nothing wrong with wanting to go fast. But going fast without control is a killer. So many riders get on the track and don't recognize the importance of this subtle balance. Riding on the track is like being set loose in a candy store. Keeping the balance—recognizing Jekyll and Hyde within yourself—takes forethought, concentration, and practice.

I have a saying: "You must slow down to go fast." You need to have the patience to do it right before you can do it fast. Frequently at school people describe a problem with a certain corner, and start by saying, "Well, I came into it a little too fast and . . ." Stop right there! They've just described the problem. They need to slow down. They know it themselves, but they won't listen to the voice in their heads. If that voice is telling you to slow down, then slow down.

I understand that people come to CLASS to test their limits, and within reason, I encourage this. It's human nature, and it's part of the learning process. But at the same time they must temper their exuberance with discipline. Things can go awry very quickly when their abilities are not adequate for the speed they're carrying.

Let me give you an example. Once a guy came to school on a powerful new V-twin. He told me ahead of time that he and his friends were "fast guys" and they wanted to be sure CLASS wasn't too mild for them. We discussed

I HAVE A SAYING: "YOU MUST SLOW DOWN TO GO FAST." *You need to have the patience to do it right before you can do it fast. (Ian Donald Photography)*

it and they decided to join us. By 10:30 am he'd gone down in a slow-entry sweeper that gets very fast on the exit. He broke his front brake lever and wasn't able to get it replaced until the next day, but he hung around to observe the school and be with his friends.

After a couple of hours he commented to an instructor: "I notice a lot of people go really fast through the turns, but not super-fast on the straights. That seems backward to me." The instructor grinned and replied, "They have the patience to work on technique, rather than pure speed. They know that if you slow down to go fast, the rest will follow." It's easy to go fast on the straightaway. But it takes control, and practice, to be fast in the corners.

CONSISTENCY: GETTING IT RIGHT EVERY TIME

One of the ways I challenge my students is on their consistency—or lack of it. I've known a lot of my students for a long time, and some of them can get around the track very fast. But one of the things that makes me faster, and safer, is my consistency.

I define consistency as the ability to repeat a certain exercise properly, over and over. You should constantly critique yourself and strive to be better. Don't repeat bad habits.

Consistency doesn't come naturally. It's learned. For instance, students might string together three or four good corners using the correct line, weight shift, and throttle control—but

MY ROOTS IN MOTORCYCLING

My attitude toward motorcycling —the emphasis on control, smoothness, and lifelong learning—started in the small town of Hornchurch, outside London.

The year is 1955. By day, I am working in a motorcycle shop. The few pounds ($25) per week are enough to buy some parts in the hopes of adding a few more mph to my 1951 350cc Triumph 3T. Like all my mates, I am chasing the elusive "ton," 100 mph.

By night, I am riding, talking, breathing motorcycles. By the time I change my clothes from work and pull up to the famed ACE Cafe, there are more than 100 bikes assembled outside. Before the night is through, we will visit three other cafes for what we call a "frothy coffee run." Eventually, the talk turns to speed, and the next step is as inevitable as the London rain: Someone says, "wheel it out, mate," and we take to the streets.

Life is reduced to its essential elements. There is unbridled enthusiasm, a single-minded focus, and most important, tremendous pleasure in doing something well.

Even at 15, I knew I wanted a bike. Predictably, my parents oppose this, but since I am working up to three jobs—at the butcher, the green grocer, and anywhere else I could pick up a few pounds sterling—I am released to buy the 3T. (I also hock my watch.)

The first ride is to the insurance agent, in the pouring rain. No sooner have I put the bike up on the stand, than a policeman comes by, notices that the bike is not licensed, and gives me a ticket. My excuse—that I am there to purchase insurance in order to obtain a license—is to no avail. Later that week, I celebrate ownership by giving my mother a ride home from the hairdresser. By the time we get home, she needs to have her hair done again. Great Memories. (Sorry Mum.)

It doesn't take long before my passion becomes my work, and I am one of eight mechanics working in a local shop. This allows me to lay my hands on the fastest machines of the day: BSA A10 Road Rockets, Matchless G11s, and Royal Enfield Constellations.

Soon I am eyeing another, quicker bike: a '53 650cc Triumph Thunderbird—the last year of the infamous sprung hub with its watch-like complexity. No sooner do I have it then I want to make it faster. The search for a few more mph is a never-ending one for my mates and me.

Though the country is rebuilding from a devastating war and money is scarce, we make do. Improvisation becomes an art form. I fabricate my own clip-on handlebars, mimicking the bend used by a favorite racer. I move the pegs higher, and farther back, attaining a racer's crouch. I grind the inlet and exhaust ports, and add a second carburetor.

But these things are not enough. You can never do enough. I locate a set of coveted Ferodo green brake linings and drill, countersink, and rivet them in place. I tweak the primitive suspension. I remove the generator to save drag on the motor, which necessitates a "total-loss" electrical system that is sufficient to run the bike and its minimalist lights for a few hours. All the while, the object is simply this: to go faster than the other guy.

Each night at the ACE Cafe, or Ma Johnson's, the drill is usually the same, as long as the weather is good. Three or four of us make the "big entrance," announced by the sound of our sharp-running British twins. A group rushes over to inspect the changes and upgrades made since we met last. It is a form of competitiveness, to be sure, and yet somehow there is no jealousy or bad intent. We are just motorcyclists, talking the talk, asserting our bragging rights over meat pies and a cup of tea. Hot memories.

Before long, the talk escalates, and the call comes down: "Wheel it out, mate." In front of Ma Johnson's is a long straight. One or two at a time, we come through at 100-plus—it's called the magic ton, and we later got to be known as the "ton-up boys."

My own personal best, riding the Thunderbird, is 108 mph. This is enough to convey bragging rights, for a while. In our group, the formula is simple, unpretentious—the guy that gets the most respect is the guy that goes the fastest. People come over to look at my bike and try to determine the mechanical magic behind it. I try not to seem boastful or egotistical, but inside, I am basking in my accomplishment: a good feeling.

Every night, a new memory is born. A guy tries to teach his girlfriend to ride in the ACE parking lot, but she dumps the clutch, bumps another bike, and 12 meticulously fettled motorcycles go down like dominoes. Another night at the ACE someone puts a record on the jukebox, and the challenge is to ride down the road, go through a tunnel, around a roundabout, and get back before the song is over. (It was tough to beat Elvis.) We are riding at night, in the wet, and even in the snow.

Only slowly do we begin to perceive danger. One night, late, I am rounding a bend and the muffler touches down. The back end lifts, and the bike launches me into a fence. Across the street, a group is waiting for the bus, and they see the whole thing, wondering if I am dead. I am not wearing a helmet. My boot is ground away on one side, and my ankle bone shows through. The bike is unrideable. I remember pushing it home, bleeding badly.

Another time, a car in front of me pulls out to pass when I am going 100-plus with my girlfriend on the back. I am able to take care of business, but it puts a scare into me. Incidents like that have me thinking: Maybe it's time I take my passion to the track. This single thought marks the beginning of my racing career.

Would I have done it any differently, looking back? Perhaps. But I don't think so. Behavior like that would be madness today, given the traffic density, and the conduct of today's drivers. Back then, there was a certain courtesy on the roadways. Motorcycles were ubiquitous,

My love of motorcycling started in Hornchurch, outside London. In those days my mates and I lived and breathed motorcycles. With a little fettling, I was able to eke 108 mph out of this '53 650cc Triumph Thunderbird (left). All of it—the danger, the adventure, the camaraderie—lives on in me today, a wellspring of good feelings. (Photo courtesy Reg Pridmore)

and were afforded respect in a way that is not the case today.

All of it—the danger, the adventure, the camaraderie—lives on in me today, a wellspring of good feelings. I realize, too, that a theme runs through it all: an openness to learning. Motorcycling is a puzzle so vast you can never complete it all.

I'm more experienced now, but I'm still working on the puzzle today.

These are my roots in motorcycling; the foundation of my attitude, my respect, my love of the sport. I took chances, and in the end I was lucky, and I learned from it. But those days live on in me every day. Life was good then!

As soon as you start feeling really good, step back and re-evaluate your riding!

Tall, laconic Fred Willink is a fixture at most CLASS sessions. Many students have watched in amazement as he pilots his huge Honda Gold Wing around the track at speeds that most students could only hope to achieve on featherweight sportbikes. Willink's infatuation with bikes started when he sat on his father's Indian as a child. However, he didn't start racing until he was in his 50s. Now he competes in a variety of displacement classes. "I do OK," he says, "but the hope of winning is not why I race. I just enjoy it."

Willink attended his first CLASS in 1989, and has been an instructor since '95. In his long riding career, Willink has had his share of close calls and surprises. Through them all, he's learned the value of keeping his emotions in check. More important, he treats each one as a learning opportunity. Here are his tips on controlling your emotions.

ON PANIC:

"Most riders come to CLASS to learn specific techniques. But they also take home something else: an encounter with panic. By the end of the day they are experimenting with their limits, and they will almost inevitably have a 'moment of concern.' This can be incredibly valuable. The more they experience these situations, the more they can learn to overcome them. When their bikes start to slide, or they do something careless, they are

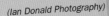
(Ian Donald Photography)

forced to deal with the consequences of their actions. I try to emphasize that these moments should always be treated as valuable learning activities. It's a matter of perspective.

"I'm not saying that riders should seek out these situations. But if they do experience such moments, the lessons learned can pay big dividends on the street, where it really counts. For instance, when a car pulls in front of you, you'll be able to use the skills you've developed, such as smooth braking and body steering. In contrast, someone who succumbs to panic might just stamp on the rear brake and lay the bike down.

ON READING THE SIGNS:

"It's possible to take a lot of the 'panic' out of a panic situation by keying in to your surroundings. For instance, let's say you see a bunch of skid marks in the road as you enter a corner. This might provide a clue that it's a decreasing-radius. Having read the signs, by the time you're into it, you've already begun to use the skills you've developed. It may be a situation that demands strong corrective action, but you've taken a lot of the element of surprise out of it already.

"Or say you're on an unfamiliar road, riding at a sporting pace. Just as you enter what looks like an 80 mph sweeper, you see a 45 mph sign with an arrow. You need to key in on that. As soon as you do, the situation becomes one in which you are exercising control. You're taking action; it's not something that's being done to you. Once you let your emotions take over, you've lost control.

ON EGO:

"Ego can get you into trouble. At one time I used to do a lot of endurance racing. It was a lot of fun, resulted in a lot of track time, and did a lot to build my confidence. But confidence is a form of ego. What often happened is that I would go endurance racing on Saturday, get overconfident, and fall down on Sunday. A rule of thumb: As soon as you start feeling really good, step back and re-evaluate your riding!"

how many of them could do five out of five perfectly? How many of them could do the same corner perfectly three times in a row? It's not as easy as it sounds.

Discipline is one of the keys to consistency. Being a good racer requires lots of discipline: the discipline to train and stay in race form, the discipline to do what it takes on the racetrack, and the discipline to stay as safe as possible. It takes discipline to hold back rather than try to pass when the stakes are too high. It takes discipline to stay focused and tell yourself: "This is where I need to be, in this gear, and this is where I begin my turn." You need discipline to hit your shift and brake markers at the same place each lap. When you go beyond these markers, you do so deliberately, as a means to study the effects. In this way discipline provides a foundation from which to experiment—a path to self-knowledge. If you are disciplined enough to know your exact cornering line, then you can begin to experiment with a second

or third line. In a race, this provides a means to pass or outwit your competition.

On the street, discipline means positioning yourself in a way that makes you visible to other vehicles at all times. It means always maintaining the right rpms to accelerate out of a bad situation. It means constantly painting a picture of what might happen around the next corner. In a blind right-hander, you need to imagine the biggest, ugliest thing possible waiting for you around that bend. This way, you can meet any challenge that's ahead.

Focus is another key. Often on the road or track, our thoughts are in the wild blue yonder. We're thinking about what's for dinner, family matters, or our jobs. There are times when you can get away with this—but there are times when it will bite you. I actually have students say to me: "I think my attention is pretty good. Out of all the laps I did today, I only overcooked turn 11

TOP RIDERS LIKE JASON PRIDMORE KNOW THAT GOOD RIDING TAKES DISCIPLINE. *This includes the discipline to know when to pass, and when to hold back. It takes discipline to stay focused and tell yourself, "This is where I need to be, in this gear, and this is where I begin my turn." (Ian Donald Photography)*

MOST PEOPLE THINK THEY HAVE THEIR EGOS IN CHECK. *But to me, anyone who thinks that way is already in danger. Do you think you have it all under control, and that nothing is going to happen to you? If so, my message is, watch out. Even the best, like Aaron Yates, get surprised from time to time. (Ian Donald Photography)*

STAYING HUMBLE

I've been humbled many times on a motorcycle. I've also seen many other riders humbled, sometimes with grave consequences. I meet riders all the time that have very high opinions of themselves. As far as I'm concerned, there's no place for that attitude in motorcycling. Wearing scuffed leathers may be a badge of courage to some, but it's not worth the price you may have to pay—and pay only once. No matter how competent you are, you need to know that there is an envelope in which you can ride safely, and that there's a limit to your abilities—one that can be approached very rapidly and without warning. I don't need to tell you what's on the other side . . . .

Humility is important regardless of the bike you're riding. We see some incredible machines at CLASS: fast Honda CBRs, Ducatis, Yamaha R1s, and Suzuki GSX-Rs. All have tremendous horsepower, and many are further enhanced with Power Commanders, exhaust systems, and race tires. But there's often one thing that still needs a tune-up: the rider.

EGO: THE ENEMY

I handle the word ego carefully; it offends people to think about it. Naturally, most people think they have their egos in check. But to me, anyone who thinks that way is already in danger. Do you think you have it all under control, and that nothing is going to happen to you? If so, my message is, be careful.

As you can imagine, teaching CLASS is a learning experience for my instructors and me. We've gotten to where we can see who's going to get in trouble if they don't change their ways.

Several years ago, when my son Jason was still teaching with me, we would actually pick riders we thought wouldn't make it through the day and put their names on the back of the chalkboard. We'd even tell the students that we'd done this. You'd be amazed at how this gets their attention!

I think that simple exercise helped lots of them turn on their brains and listen—they didn't want to become one of the riders on that "wall of shame." Others would fulfill our predictions by crashing. Their egos carried the day. They figured: "He couldn't be talking about me."

a few times." That's not consistency. That's absent-mindedness and complacency.

But consistency doesn't just apply to the track. You must be extra disciplined and focused on the street. Do you ever ride around without knowing what gear you're in, or with your foot poised over the rear brake? When crisis strikes and that car pulls out in front of you, these things can mean disaster. You won't have the rpms to accelerate out of danger, or you'll stab the rear brake and go into a slide. These are bad habits and you should correct them—now. Do you discipline yourself to constantly scan for upcoming hazards, such as a car pulling out of a driveway? Making the right choices in these matters can save your life.

Fortunately, it isn't this way with all our students. Many of them have been coming to CLASS for years, and some complete several days of CLASS in succession. They know that they can always learn more, and that improvement is a never-ending process. Many of these longtime riders are extremely fast, but they are also humble in the face of all there is to learn. That's the attitude that leads to a long and happy life in motorcycling.

Another example of ego's harmful effects occurs during the last few laps of the day at CLASS. By this time people are feeling good. They've been turning some good laps. They're confident and excited about their day. But it's also the danger zone. If someone is going to fall off and get hurt, that's when they seem to do it most. It's just like downhill skiing: It's always on the last run of the day, when you're feeling your best, that you break your leg.

The lesson? Don't think you can't be hurt just because you're feeling good. In fact, that's exactly when you're likely to be hurt. It's the time when a smart rider puts his ego in check and pulls back from the edge. This is where discipline comes into play; it can save you from a lot of pain and expense, and ensure that you'll be ready to have more fun tomorrow.

TRUST NO ONE

In CLASS I purposefully discourage racing against other students. This isn't because I don't want them to have fun, or that I want to part them from their competitive natures. It's because I want riders to develop their own skills, not measure themselves against others. I also don't want people placing faith in other riders by riding too close. I tell students to assume that the rider in front may not have a clue about good riding. As a rule, I don't trust anybody when I'm on a bike.

In racing, it's a different story. You have to trust the other competitors to some degree because there will be close scrapping and battling going on. But other people have caused some of my worst racing accidents. Even highly professional riders can make unexpected moves.

One example that quickly comes to mind was in '97 at the "Battle of the Legends" at

I TELL MY STUDENTS TO TRUST NO ONE. *I want them to develop their own skills, not measure themselves against others. But in rare instances—such as here, where I'm following my trusted instructor Fred Willink—it's OK to close up the gap a bit. (Ian Donald Photography)*

TALK ABOUT CLOSE RACING. *At the Battle of the Legends at Daytona, some of the top riders of our era were on identically prepared bikes. They included me (leading on 163), Gary Nixon (9), Jay Springsteen (1), Mark Brelsford (87), Dave Aldana (13), Yvon Duhamel (17), Roger Reiman (55), Don Emde (25), and Eddie Mulder (12). (Photo courtesy Rob Mitchell)*

Daytona—a great series sponsored by BMW. We were all on identically prepared bikes and I was happy to be included with some of my heroes: Gary Nixon, Yvon Duhamel, Jay Springsteen, Roger Reiman, Mark Brelsford, and others. We were going at it hard coming into one of my favorite corners: turn one. The most exciting thing about Daytona for me is going deeper than anyone else into turn one before putting on the brakes. We were three or four wide, and I was to Nixon's right on the outside. He didn't know I was there, and for some reason he suddenly moved over—right into me! I was already as far outside as I could be, and the right cylinder of his BMW twin actually lay on my left shoulder long enough to leave burn marks on my leathers. With a little luck and a lot of skill, we both stayed upright. But it was a lesson for me. Gary is one of my heroes, and someone I feel I can trust implicitly on the track. But there is an element of risk riding that close to anyone.

Ironically, I pulled something similar on him later in the same race. I was leading the pack, and Nixon decided to follow me through the chicane. Springsteen was right behind him, nose to tail. These guys are some of the best flat trackers ever—both are multi-time national champions and Hall of Fame riders. We were on the gas hard in a right–hander just before the exit of the chicane, when my rear wheel broke loose and the rear end came around to what felt like maybe a 70–degree slide!

In all my years of racing I don't remember ever having a slide like that. I didn't panic—I just kept the throttle open and managed to recover. I went through the grass and still led them up onto the banking. Nixon told me later in his gravelly voice that I could flat track with him any time!

The point is that even riders you think you can trust with your life can throw a surprise at you. When you're on a motorcycle, you can't completely trust anyone.

GETTING IN A ROUTINE

There is no such thing as a simple, no-brainer trip on a motorcycle. Every time you get on, you need to be in the moment. You may just be going to the corner for a carton of milk. You hop on, put in the key, push the starter button, and off you go. But you know what? You may be in for the biggest surprise of your life. That left-turning car could be around the next bend. Part of your routine must involve taking a moment to wake yourself up and focus on your surroundings and where you're going.

Tune your brain in. Have a little discussion with yourself every time before you ride. Even if it's just five miles to work, you need to survey the situation. It's a way of being in control. After all, you can be killed leaving your own driveway!

No single mental technique is the key to being a faster, safer motorcyclist. To be a really good rider, you need to put all these pieces together at once. It takes thought, planning, and practice. It all starts in your head.

I'M BIG ON ROUTINES. This includes everything from a quick mechanical check, to just waking yourself up to your surroundings each time you roll out the driveway. (Ian Donald Photography)

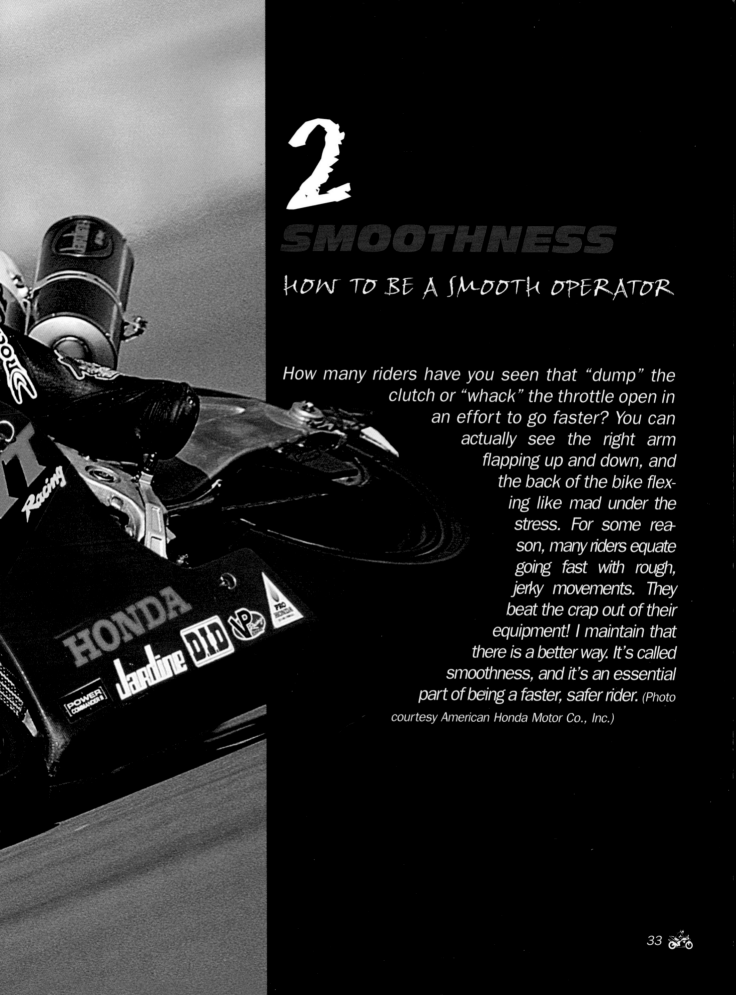

2

SMOOTHNESS

HOW TO BE A SMOOTH OPERATOR

How many riders have you seen that "dump" the clutch or "whack" the throttle open in an effort to go faster? You can actually see the right arm flapping up and down, and the back of the bike flexing like mad under the stress. For some reason, many riders equate going fast with rough, jerky movements. They beat the crap out of their equipment! I maintain that there is a better way. It's called smoothness, and it's an essential part of being a faster, safer rider. *(Photo courtesy American Honda Motor Co., Inc.)*

Smoothness will enhance your riding in ways you never thought possible. Smoothness isn't just an artful touch to add to your riding. It's an essential part of going fast, being safe, and being in *control*. It makes the bike far more responsive and predictable.

Sidecar racing made me realize the importance of being smooth. Racing these outfits is inherently dangerous, and weight transfer is critical. As the person at the controls (the "pilot"), I developed a great deal of concern for my passenger. Imagine moving around, trying to find a handhold at 125 mph! My goal was to smooth things out for the passenger, and what I

COMPLETE CLUTCH ACTION QUICKLY. *I recommend that you pull the clutch lever in about a third of its total throw, just enough to disengage it. If you pull the lever all the way to the bar, you will tend to quickly "dump" it again to engage the gear, which isn't good for smoothness, or traction.*

YOU MUST BE SMOOTH IN THE WET. *Smoothness is paramount in the rain where abrupt throttle or braking inputs can have grave consequences. Roll it on and roll it off gently! (Ian Donald Photography)*

learned had implications for all my riding. This was further reinforced when I started doing a lot of two-up riding. A passenger is a great yardstick for smoothness. If your helmets are banging together every time you shift—and your partner gives you a dour expression at the end of the ride—you can bet your smoothness needs a little work. Here are just a few situations where smoothness will help you:

Getting on the gas. Today's motorcycles, whether sportbike, touring bike, or cruiser, are all very powerful. The bigger and more powerful they are, the more respect they require. Every time you're on or off the throttle, you're giving a message to the rear wheel. If you don't give it the right message, you'll end up on the ground. This is especially true in low-speed corners. If you get on the gas too hard, the back end will step out—with predictable results.

Downshifting. If you downshift roughly, there will come a time when your bike will slide out—especially in adverse weather or in an off-camber, downhill turn. You should downshift in such a way that the rear wheel doesn't "chirp."

Any time you're not vertical. Whatever traction you have is reduced when you lean the bike over. While you may get away with rough movements and abrupt inputs on a straight road, these same actions will put you down if you do them mid-turn.

There's another, less pragmatic reason to be smooth: *it's fun.* When smoothness becomes a goal and even an art form for you, you'll find your enjoyment of the bike will skyrocket. CLASS students tell me this every day: They have more fun, and feel better about their riding, by being smooth.

There is no better feeling than moving quickly and safely while arranging all of your inputs—throttle, clutch, braking, and body movements—in one finely orchestrated symphony.

You'll also find the benefits of smoothness will carry over to other activities in your life. My son Jason, a successful racer, was reared on a philosophy of smoothness. As an adult, he's found that this approach enhances his car driving, his

bicycling—even his golf game. That's the benefit of being smooth. Ideally, all your activities should "flow," like a peaceful river.

YOU MUST WORK AT IT

Smoothness is not something you add to your riding in an afternoon. You need to pursue it and work hard. You can *always* be smoother.

People tell me I'm a very smooth rider. But after almost 50 years of riding and racing, I still work at it—diligently. So should you. Constantly ask yourself: How smoothly can I work the clutch, or the brakes? How can I make my riding "flow?" These are ongoing challenges for all of us. The potential rewards are great.

ELEMENTS OF SMOOTHNESS

When I think of the critical components of smoothness, four things come to mind: throttle, clutch, braking, and body movement. We'll go over these topics in detail elsewhere in this book,

but here's an explanation of each as it directly relates to smoothness.

1. THROTTLE

If you watch World Superbike or MotoGP racing on TV, you can see the black rubber marks the riders lay down as they exit corners. This indicates how much power these bikes have. It's sufficient to spin the back wheel at will.

Modern street bikes differ only in degree; a twist of the throttle still generates phenomenal power. On the street, you need to be constantly thinking about the ramifications of this. You need to monitor your emotions. Apply a little too much of that intoxicating horsepower, and you'll be down.

Think of throttle action as being on a gradient: not as an on/off switch. If you're sitting at a light and hit the throttle as hard as you can, you'll either spin the rear wheel or pick up the front in a wheelie. The idea is to find a balance: *Roll* on the

AT AN EXTREME LEAN ANGLE, SMOOTHNESS IS CRITICAL . *While you may get away with rough movements and abrupt inputs on a straight road, these same actions will put you down if you do them mid-turn. (Ian Donald Photography)*

FROM RIDING A STONE AXE

Where does smoothness come from? For many, it's a cultivated skill, acquired for reasons of safety, speed, or maybe just to be a classier-looking rider. Certainly, these are legitimate reasons.

For me, as a racer in the '70s, it was a matter of survival, plain and simple. Smoothness was part of my race kit, like a good set of leathers. I didn't become smooth for high-minded reasons, or to impress anyone, or for bragging rights. I did it as a means of self-preservation.

My smooth riding techniques started as far back as 1965, when I had a horrific crash (resulting in a double compound fracture, broken ribs, broken collarbone, and a fractured skull). It was then that I began to formulate my philosophy of smoothness and control. I decided I couldn't fight the bike. I had to work with it, using the controls and body inputs in a natural manner.

Imagine, for a moment, that the year is '77. I'm riding a Kawasaki KZ1000. The hulking 1,046cc, four-cylinder motor has been tuned to make more than 140 horsepower (measured on the famous Axtell rear-wheel dynamometer). But here is the twist: This angry lump is wrapped in an almost whimsically flexible double-down tube frame. The spindly, 34mm forks bend and sway under braking and cornering loads. The bikes quickly earn the nickname, "flexi-flyers." There is no fairing and only a small handlebar, making speeds of 140-plus a perfect opportunity to practice great body input. (These speeds were routinely achieved at Riverside and Ontario raceways in California. I reached 150-plus at Daytona, Florida, and Pocono, Pennsylvania.) This twitchy package—propelled by an explosive motor—means that any throttle,

braking, and steering inputs must be made with a deft touch. At the fastest speeds it's near impossible to lift my hands off the bar, because before I can grasp the levers, the wind forces my fingers back.

It was a monster, plain and simple. How did I deal with it? My philosophy was to let the bike have its own head. What else could I do? If I tried to manhandle it, I'd end up on the ground. Take a track like Sears Point, for instance. In what's known as the "Esses"—a series of quick right-left turns, with elevation loss —the big KZ had a tendency to do what it wanted. The front end would push pretty bad. If I rolled off the throttle at a corner entry, the front would just drop away. Sometimes it would move and I'd think, "It's not coming back this time." But it would. I had to be smooth in all my transitions, use my knee as an

For me, smoothness was a necessity, borne of riding flexible bikes like the Kawasaki KZ1000, which was tuned to produce 140 hp. Any throttle, braking, and steering inputs had to be made with a deft touch. Here I'm leading my perennial challenger Steve McLaughlin. (Photo courtesy John Ulrich)

My highly tuned KZ1000 was featured on the cover of the November 1978 issue of Cycle, with the more sedate showroom version of the bike in the background. Because of the spindly forks and double-down tube frame, the bikes quickly earned the nickname, "flexi-flyers." Despite lacking a fairing, the KZ achieved speeds in excess of 140 mph. (Photo courtesy Hachette Filipacchi Magazines)

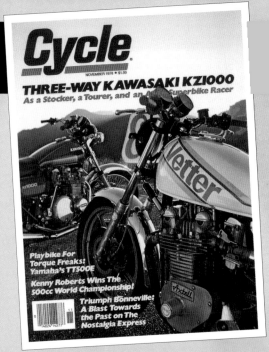

outrigger, and try not to tighten up or panic.

The big Kawi wasn't the only bike that forced me to exercise a gentle touch. The BMW R90S, which I rode from '74 to '76, was another classroom for dedication and smoothness. Here was a bike that had been brought to the thin-edge of reliability with titanium connecting rods, hollow valve lifters, hollow titanium pushrods, and a host of other modifications that made it fast but fragile. The transmission was a little antiquated, and would come apart if you were rough on it. Stock rpm limit was about 7,000, but we used to coax as much as 9 grand out of the motor in order to generate peak power, with no rev limiter, of course!

People called it a grenade, ready to explode. But the trick to dealing with a grenade is to not pull the pin, or, if you must pull the pin, *put it back very gently*. And that was accomplished with smoothness and dedication. I had to be in touch with the motor and chassis at all times, and monitor all my inputs in the correct manner.

Those old bikes would scare the heck out of anyone accustomed to today's great sportbikes. These days, the bikes do a lot of the work for you. Sometimes I feel lucky that I was self-trained 30 years ago, when control and smoothness meant everything. Riding those old bikes was the perfect preparation for the powerful machines we have today. You still have to manage the phenomenal power of today's bikes very carefully, but in general, they have far more capability than most riders can use.

When I think back, I realize that in every era, riders have struggled to master the capabilities of their machines. It amazes me to think that the Isle of Man TT is almost 100 years old. Those first riders, on their flat-tank Nortons and Triumphs, would probably think I had it easy racing in the '70s, in the same way that I am amazed at the capabilities of today's sportbikes.

Where does it all end? Thankfully, it never does. We all make the best of what we have. That is the artistry and the beauty of our sport. We try, sometimes we fail or fall down, but we move on, and we learn. It's the learning that counts, and I try never to forget that, no matter what I'm riding. Experience is the teacher.

THINK OF THROTTLE ACTION AS BEING ON A GRADIENT —NOT AS AN ON/OFF SWITCH. *The action is like that of a "rocking horse." If you're rolling on the throttle, you should be easing off the brake. If you're squeezing the brake, you should be rolling off the throttle, the two actions flowing seamlessly together.*

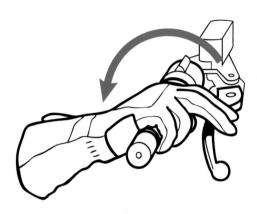

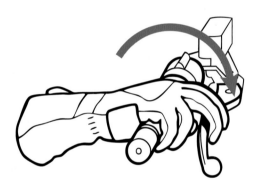

throttle, and *feed* in the clutch. Don't snap open the throttle or dump the clutch—whether you're leaving a light, coming out of a turn, or accelerating up a straightaway.

Here's a specific technique for gripping the throttle that will help you "roll it on." Start by placing your third and fourth fingers around the throttle. Then place the first and second fingers on the front brake lever. I "cover" the brake this way 90 percent of the time I'm riding. With your fingers in this position, the action is like that of a "rocking horse"; If you're rolling on the throttle, you should be easing off the brake. If you're

squeezing the brake, you should be rolling off the throttle. These two actions should flow seamlessly into one another. It takes practice to get it right, but after a while it will become second nature. And it's the smoothest way.

It's also important to relax your hand and arm muscles. You shouldn't have any tension on the twistgrip. Grip tension not only causes fatigue, it makes your throttle action abrupt. To address this, consciously relax the muscles of your hands and forearms several times during a ride. With your hands relaxed in this way, you can manage the throttle in fine increments, which is what you want.

One more thing: If you think this type of smooth acceleration is just for street riding, think again. It's also the fastest way to accelerate on the track. Once, to improve my racing starts, I went to the drag strip and trained with fellow superbike racer Cook Neilson. What I learned was that I needed more control—and more smoothness—to keep the front end down and maintain traction. The best racers, poised at the start of a MotoGP with almost 200 horsepower at their disposal, know the value of being smooth with the throttle.

2. CLUTCH

In the past, during the afternoon at a typical CLASS session, I used to give rides on the back of my bike. Most students achieve lean angles they've never experienced before! Of course, my goal isn't to scare them, but to try to impress them with how smoothly a motorcycle can be ridden at a fairly good clip.

The first and most common response is: "Where did you get that automatic transmission?" They don't feel the shifts; they just hear the engine note change. You should strive for the same thing.

So much of this has to do with how you use the clutch. You need to pull it in smoothly, and release it smoothly, especially during downshifts. Here's how:

Don't pull the clutch all the way to the bar.
I recommend that you pull the lever in about one-third of its total throw—just enough to disengage it. If you pull the lever all the way to the bar, you'll tend to quickly "dump" it again to engage the gear: not good for smoothness, or traction.

If you don't give the rear wheel the right message, you'll end up on the ground. Today's motorcycles—whether sportbike, touring bike, or cruiser—are all very powerful. The bigger and more powerful they are, the more respect they require. (Ian Doanld Photography)

STATIC DRILLS

There's a lot you can teach yourself about smoothness, control, and other riding skills without ever leaving your garage. I call this "static training," and it's something I've done throughout my career.

I first began using static drills at the starting line in races. I always made sure I was left alone for a minute in order to visualize a quick lap in my mind. I'd see myself getting a good start and holding off everyone through the first turn. Then I'd envision the next few turns, ensuring that I didn't do something stupid on cold tires. This kind of visualization gave me a lot of confidence.

At other times I'd envision a start that was less than ideal, perhaps where I was fourth or fifth and was really being pushed. Then the challenge was to maintain my composure and not become flustered. I'd play all these scenarios through in my mind, the good and the bad, without any risk of being hurt.

Anyone can perform visualization techniques before a track day. You can envision every detail, in every turn: speed, gear, track position, and the use of the controls. For instance, you might see yourself coming around Turn 11 at Laguna Seca, accelerating under the bridge, taking Turn 1 at speed, downshifting, and braking for Turn 2. You can practice the smallest throttle and control movements. It's possible to do several laps this way and get yourself in order before ever taking to the track.

You can also practice control and body movements statically. One very useful drill is to gently squeeze the front brake as discussed in Chapter 3, then release it just as gently. You can also practice the "rocking horse" motion with your right hand: Whenever you're off the throttle, you're on the brake. And whenever you're off the brake, you're on the throttle.

Body steering also lends itself to static practice. Sit on your bike, relax the top half of your body, bend your elbows, and move across the centerline in the desired direction. As you gain confidence, you can start moving the cheek of your bum off the saddle, toward the desired corner (right for right-hand turns, left for left-handers). Also, practice weighting the inside peg to help turn the bike. Evaluate your body movements while you're on the stand. Is your head lined up with your inside wrist, instead of over the "high side" of the bike? Is your outside inner knee pulling on the gas tank through the turn? Is your outside elbow relaxed? Are you able to be symmetrical going to the right or to the left?

Street riding can also be practiced statically. Envision a traffic situation, such as a car pulling out from a side street in front of you. What will you do? Will you stomp on the rear brake and go into a slide, or will you apply the front brake in a smooth, controlled fashion and avoid an accident? A little practice in the garage could make all the difference.

You can learn a lot sitting still! Even during the height of my racing career, I practiced static drills. Here I'm showing students how to practice getting set up for a corner by moving the body, arms, and head. (Ian Donald Photography)

Err on the side of more rpms. In CLASS I draw an enormous one-foot tachometer on the board and tell people: *rpms are your friend.* It's one of my golden rules. So much of good clutch technique involves "matching" rpms to your speed. When you pull in the clutch, don't let the rpms drop or the engine will become a brake, and you'll risk locking the back wheel. Your engine speed should be at least at the same level as when you pulled the clutch in.

Even better, elevate your rpms above that level (*blip* the throttle), so by the time you complete the shift and let the clutch back out, the rpms are about where they were when you started the shift. What does this mean in terms of numbers? My recommendations might surprise you. For a modern four-cylinder sportbike, I recommend 6,000–12,000 rpm; for a pushrod twin such as a BMW, I recommend 4,000–6,000 rpm; and for a Ducati V-twin, it's 6,000–8,000 rpm. You needn't worry about hurting your motor—bikes are meant to be ridden this way. Try it, and I have no doubt that rpms will help your smoothness.

Do it *right now.* Don't be lackadaisical about your clutch work. Master the timing so you can do it quickly, but smoothly. Don't procrastinate!

3. BRAKING

Many riders treat the front brake as an on/off switch. They just grab it. Too often, this means they lock up the wheel, lay the bike down, and slide under a vehicle.

You need to "get in touch" with your brakes and know them intimately. Think of the front brake as your friend. (We'll discuss front vs. rear brakes in the next chapter.) Today's bikes offer fantastic braking, but every machine is different. Whether you're riding a single-disc 250cc standard or a 1000cc double-disc sportbike, you need to learn how much braking power you have and how to regulate it. The initial squeeze should be gentle: just enough to achieve contact between the pads and rotor. Then you should squeeze it progressively harder, as needed. Be very conscious of the amount of pressure you're applying, and its effects. This takes practice in a safe environment. (In the next chapter, I'll explain some specific braking drills that we use

SMOOTH CLUTCH-WORK. *This rider is smoothly transitioning through a tight left hander. Study the shot and imagine how well he's managing by keeping the rpms up in a lower gear. At the same time he's got control, not only with the throttle, but also by slipping the clutch just slightly to maintain smoothness. (Kevin Wing Photography)*

FOR SMOOTHNESS WHEN SHIFTING, YOUR ENGINE SPEED SHOULD BE AT LEAST AT THE SAME LEVEL AS WHEN YOU PULLED THE CLUTCH IN. *Even better, elevate your rpms above that level, so by the time you complete the shift and let the clutch back out, the rpms are about where they were when you started the shift. Rpms are your friend! It's one of my golden rules. When you pull in the clutch, don't let the rpms drop or the engine will become a brake, and you'll risk locking the back wheel.*

NICKY KNOWS SMOOTH

A good racer knows that smoothness is a key ingredient to speed. Nicky Hayden is one of the great up and coming champions of our day. He's won both AMA 600 Supersport and Superbike Championships here in the states, and has quickly risen to the MotoGP ranks on the factory Honda team where we're watching him improve with every race.

I've enjoyed watching Nicky race since he was 16 and I've had the pleasure of riding with him on the track when he joined me for a CLASS at Sears Point Raceway a while back. Nicky is a very smooth rider and as his experience grows, he gets smoother.

I read an article recently where Nicky was talking about being the rookie on the team with multi-time world champ Valentino Rossi. One key to his learning is to watch what his teammate does. His comments were that he marveled at how smooth Rossi was on certain sections of the track where Nicky was still learning. Even though Nicky's probably one of the smoothest riders in the world, he knows he needs to be smoother to be faster.

It's been great to watch Nicky Hayden's steady progression in pro racing. He has all the right ingredients to be a world champion one day, and I believe he'll get there. (Photo courtesy Reg Pridmore)

in CLASS.) I even recommend practicing while at a stoplight: Apply the brake lightly, and squeeze harder and harder.

OK you ask: "What good is a gentle squeeze when that SUV turns left in front of me at 40 mph?" Believe it or not, smooth braking works as well for panic stops as it does for scrubbing off a little speed. Racers make demands on their brakes that most riders will never experience, yet they cultivate smooth braking technique, because they know it will keep them upright when they need to go from 175 mph to 30 mph for a hairpin turn.

Think of it this way: You're either in control or out of control. If you've trained yourself to brake smoothly, you'll brake smoothly in every situation. You need to get yourself in an emotional position where you won't grab the front brake—even in an emergency. It's like practicing for any emergency: If you don't prepare, you won't react properly.

One key technique to smooth front braking is using just two fingers. Many instructors emphatically teach the use of four fingers, but with modern bikes, two fingers are adequate and this method will encourage you to use the brakes with moderation. Also, don't "dump" the brake when you're done with it. Try to feed the brake back out as smoothly as you applied it. Learning how to modulate the brake in this way—squeezing it gently, and releasing it gently—will help you maintain traction and keep your bike settled and stable.

4. BODY

I'm sure you've all seen racers "hanging off" their bikes in corners. This isn't theatrics. Even on the street, body movement will help you get around corners smoothly and safely. When your input comes from the whole body, you're reducing tension on your arms. Tension causes abrupt movements and overreaction. To be smooth, you need to move your body.

A lot of riders are cautious about moving around over the bike at speeds greater than 50 mph. I recommend starting by just moving the top half of the body, positioning your chin at an angle approximately lined up with the right wrist for a right turn, or the left wrist for a left turn.

Keep your arms relaxed. When this becomes comfortable, take one more step and move the lower half of your body. Imagine a pivot point in the hollow of your crotch, right where the tank ends. Pivot slightly right or left around this point, weight the inside peg, and see if this doesn't help take the bike around the corner for "free." The bike will help you if you give it the chance!

If you have that little sequence together—and it may seem like a lot to some—you'll find that the bike will work for you rather than against you. I encourage you to add body movement a little at a time.

You should consciously relax your body. Tension usually starts at the shoulders and upper back, which induces stress all the way down the arms and to the hands. Drop your shoulders and relax. A lot of riders also get rigid and hold their breath as they enter corners. As you can imagine, this tenses every muscle in the body.

Be sure to breathe!

SMOOTHNESS COUNTS.
Great racers like Nicky Hayden or Ben Bostrom (pictured) smoothly shift their body weight to the inside of the bike in a turn. Hanging off with your knee on the ground is the more advanced end of the spectrum, but weight shifts can help riders at any level corner better. (Photo courtesy American Honda Motor Co., Inc.)

3

BRAKING

THE ART OF SLOWING DOWN

I've always loved braking. As a racer, I prided myself on being able to go deeper into a corner than most of the other guys. I knew my brakes intimately and how to get every last bit of performance out of them. It was something I worked on very hard. (Ian Donald Photography)

BRAKE CHECK. *There will come a time when you need to extract every last bit of performance from your brakes. When this time comes, your life will depend on the skills you have developed.*

Every racer knows that braking is a learned skill. As with virtually everything in motorcycling, you need to practice to become proficient. Unfortunately, this is *not* the way most riders approach braking. Most use what I call the "grab-and-stab" approach. They figure they'll just wait for something to happen, and the brakes will be there for them. When riders tell me this, I want to shake them! Some even say, "I've been riding a long time and I've never had anything bad happen." Maybe so, but do you want to just wait for something to happen? Or will you *prepare* for the eventuality?

Believe me, there will come a time when you need to extract every last bit of performance from your brakes. It might be next week, or it might be next month—but you *will* be presented with a situation that requires maximum braking. And when this moment comes, your life will depend on the skills you've developed. You need to devise scenarios in advance that you can respond to with controlled braking—and then practice, practice, practice.

THE FRONT BRAKE DOES THE BUSINESS

Some people tell me they never use the front brake because they fear an "endo" or some other catastrophe. That's frightening to hear, because it's the front brake that does almost all the business of slowing the motorcycle down.

Here's why: When the brakes are applied, the weight of you and your bike is pitched forward. This provides more traction on the front wheel, which allows you to apply more braking, and so on. The rear wheel doesn't experience this increase in traction—in fact, the rear is *lightened* during braking, which is why it's so easy to lock up the rear wheel and skid. Minimum stopping distance, as shown in hundreds of braking tests, can only occur through the use of the front brake.

The front brake is so effective that sometimes it seems you can drive the front wheel into the ground. At the limits of braking, you can hear the front tire howl—a sort of tearing sound when you're in the saddle.

Racers are familiar with this noise, because it marks the limit of how far they can go before the wheel slides away. They have a fine-tuned feel for how much the front tire can be loaded. Like them, you should become familiar with the limits of braking. It could mean the difference between avoiding something or slamming into it.

For people who are apprehensive about using the front brake, my message is simply this: Explore it a little at a time, in an upright position. It's very possible to confront this fear and overcome it. The confidence and safety you will gain will be worth the effort.

THE RIGHT POSITION FOR THE RIGHT HAND

Proper use of the front brake starts with good hand and finger position. I teach people to let the first and second fingers "float" over the front brake lever. If you haven't been doing this up to now, it may take some getting used to. But it's the best way to ensure instantaneous braking response. Some instructional programs recommend using four fingers on the brake lever. This is a personal choice, but I find that most modern brakes can be adequately modulated with just two fingers.

Most modern brake levers allow you to "dial in" the reach to position them closer or farther from the bar when at rest. Use this adjustment according to your hand size, ensuring that your index and middle fingers can wrap comfortably around the lever. However, be careful not to reduce reach so much that the lever hits the bar under hard braking.

COVERING THE BRAKE

When I'm riding, I "cover" the front brake 90 percent of the time by resting two fingers on the lever. In an urban situation, I cover it 100 percent of the time. I don't want to lose *any* reaction time under those circumstances. In the milliseconds it takes you to remove your fingers from the twistgrip and place them on the brake lever, you can travel 20–30 feet. This can mean the difference between stopping safely and slamming into the car in front of you.

THE ROCKING HORSE

Early in my racing career I realized that the more I could make the front brake and throttle work in harmony, the more stable and smooth the bike would be. It's a matter of giving the motorcycle the right "message." Here's how it works in a nutshell: *Whenever I'm off the throttle, I'm on the brake. And whenever I'm off the brake, I'm on the throttle.* I call this the rocking horse motion.

TOP. *I cover the front brake 90 percent of the time by resting two fingers on the lever. In an urban situation, I cover it 100 percent of the time. I don't want to lose any reaction time.*

BOTTOM. *The front brake does almost all the business of stopping, and today's double disks are so powerful they make it seem like you can drive the front wheel into the ground.*

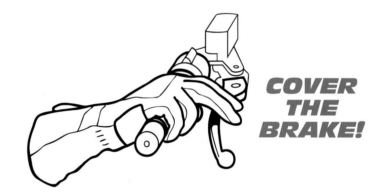

COVER THE BRAKE!

BRAKING DRILL

At CLASS we do a braking drill just before the lunch break. Here's how it works: Students form several lines, with an instructor standing ahead of them, 100 feet away. The instructor indicates which brake you should use—one hand up means use the front brake only; lifting a foot in the air means use the rear brake only; and a hand and foot up means use both brakes. After indicating which brake to use, the instructor signals for you to accelerate forward. When you reach the instructor, you should apply the brake in a smooth, controlled fashion. The goal is to understand the value of front brake alone, the rear brake alone, and of course both together. You perform each exercise for 10 minutes.

The emphasis is smoothness. Our instructors aren't looking for you to stop on a dime, the ability to lock up the wheel, or a nifty "stoppie" (front wheel stand). They're simply critiquing how you apply the brakes.

When we use this drill in CLASS, it offers amazing insights. The first and most remarkable thing occurs when we ask students to use the front brake only—more than half will stab the rear brake instead! They tell us it's a force of habit.

The other thing we see is rough application of the front brake. We're looking for the elusive rocking horse effect: simultaneously rolling off of the throttle and squeezing the lever. Instead, what we frequently see is a rough grab for the lever, as indicated by extreme fork dive (compression). I tell people to imagine that a glass of liquid is balanced on the fairing, and their job is not to spill it under braking. People ask me, "Doesn't this mean you won't stop as fast?" I say no—smooth braking is optimum braking, from any speed.

Strange mating ritual? No, it's the CLASS braking drill! One hand up means use the front brake only; lifting a foot in the air means use the rear brake only; and a hand and foot up means use both brakes. The emphasis is on smoothness. (Ian Donald Photography)

This may take time to master, but when you get it, you won't believe how it will help the motorcycle behave more smoothly. Start by practicing in the garage, where you can't be hurt. Develop a gentle rolling motion with the wrist. When you accelerate, slowly release the brake. When you squeeze the brake, roll off the throttle. It's simple!

Of course, in reality there will be occasional gaps between the two actions (braking and acceleration). But I try to "seal" them up as tightly as possible. This gives the motorcycle a much better message than grabbing the brake or slamming the throttle open. This rocking horse movement also has a settling effect on the suspension, which is why it's used so much in racing. It stabilizes the bike.

OTHER MEANS OF DECELERATION: ROLLING OFF THE THROTTLE VS. DOWNSHIFTING

A lot of riders navigate the twisties by simply rolling the throttle on and off. I tend to avoid this. I always prefer to downshift. This slows me just a bit, and enables me to come back on the throttle very quickly. It puts me in a more commanding position, and keeps the rpms up. (Remember: rpms are your best friend!) I always prefer to manage a corner by accelerating through it.

I also have a "golden rule" that applies to deceleration for corners: *Downshift first, then apply the brakes.* Many people find the timing difficult if they try to brake first and then downshift. What generally happens is they try to blip the throttle for a downshift while maintaining pressure on the brake, and this hand action fluctuates the brake, unsettling the motorcycle.

As you get better, you can move braking "closer" to downshifting until you're able to do them simultaneously. It's an advanced technique but necessary for fast track riding or late braking in competition. But in general for most street riding, I recommend that you downshift first.

REAR BRAKE: WHEN TO USE IT

I'm a tireless advocate of the front brake. Nonetheless, I hate it when people tell me they never use the rear brake. Granted, it doesn't play a huge role in racing, because the rear wheel gets so light under hard braking (or even rises off the ground) that it can't supply the bulk of your

WHEN THE BRAKES ARE APPLIED, THE WEIGHT OF YOU AND YOUR BIKE IS PITCHED FORWARD. *This provides more traction on the front wheel, which allows you to apply more braking, and so on. At the limits of braking, you can hear the front tire howl, a sort of tearing sound.*

THE REAR BRAKE CAN'T SUPPLY THE BULK OF YOUR BRAKING POWER. *But it can offer the last 10 percent, and offers a stabilizing effect on the chassis. Keep your foot off the pedal so you don't stab it.*

braking power. But it can supply that last 10 percent. More importantly, it has a stabilizing effect on the chassis.

You need to understand the rear brake and its qualities. Envision the application of the rear brake "stretching" the frame. In effect, it drags the rear wheel and settles the front. Honda's LBS

POCONO 1977

In early 1977 my fruitful association with BMW came to an end, and I began riding the fast but evil-handling Racecrafters Kawasaki KZ1000, tuned by the legendary Pierre Des Roches. Des Roches had performed a variety of modifications that made the big four fast—but that took it to the ragged edge of its handling potential.

For starters, the bike was bored out to displace 1046cc. Compression and rpm limits were both raised. Several inches were removed from the left side of the engine to improve cornering clearance. Similarly, the points were moved an inch inboard on the right. Stainless steel valves were installed, and the head was reworked to improve flow tremendously.

The list of changes went on. To improve handling extra bracing was added to the steering head. The swingarm was reworked and rewelded, and the shock mounts were changed to provide a lay-down position. A host of extraneous stuff was banished to the trash heap, including electric starter, turn signal brackets, passenger footpegs, and stock battery. Every aspect of the bike was put on a diet. It was at this point that I began to see a real future in improving power-to-weight ratios!

The high-strung machine suits me. In the first races of the season I place in the top four at Daytona, Florida, Loudon, New Hampshire, and Sears Point, California. However, an outright win eludes me. Since I am the defending AMA Superbike Champion, the title is mine to lose, and this makes me work even harder to retain the title.

Late August, Pocono, Pennsylvania. First order of business: Saturday's heat race. Going into the chicane, I try to go underneath Wes Cooley's Yoshimura Kawasaki Z1, but there just isn't room. It's too late to turn left into the escape road, and too late to turn right and make the corner. I apply a tad of front brake, but at that lean angle, even a touch is too much, and in a millisecond I am down. After a brief tumble I have enough time to stand up, brush myself off, and still witness my bike still doing cartwheels across the infield. A grim sight, leading to some bad four-letter words in American and British.

The thoroughly wadded bike is transported back to the pits and into Des Roches' capable hands. The time: about 2 pm Saturday afternoon.

Tuner the late Pierre Des Roche worked his magic to make the big four very fast—but the newfound speed took the bike to the ragged edge of its handling potential. (Photo courtesy Reg Pridmore)

What follows is a mechanical marathon, as Des Roches works 20 hours straight to replace the fork, fender, triple clamps, head bearings, handlebars, control cables, tires, headlight assembly, number plate, oil cooler, and tailpiece. For good measure, new camshafts are installed. By 10 am Sunday, the "midnight flog," as it later became known, is complete and the bike is ready—or as ready as it will ever be.

The good news is that I feel fine and the bike is magically whole again. The bad news is that, having crashed out of the heat race, I must start at the back of the grid—not a magical position.

Fortunately, the bike is even better after the Des Roches all-nighter. Plus, I am motivated to redeem myself after the disastrous heat race. Within the first few corners, I've worked my way through half the field. Des Roches' work has paid off, and the bike sings when coming off the banking in fifth gear,

In early 1977 my fruitful association with BMW came to an end, and I began riding the fast but evil-handling Racecrafters Kawasaki KZ1000. Later that year, at Pocono, I wadded the bike in practice but came back to win the race. Very satisfying! (Photos courtesy Reg Pridmore)

screaming along the main straightaway at 10–12,000 rpm.

By the second or third lap, I'm in the lead, having passed Cooley, Yvon Duhamel (Kawasaki), and Mike Baldwin (works Moto Guzzi). I go on to win by more than 20 seconds, averaging more than 90 mph. To this day I'm not sure how I pulled it out, coming from the back like that—but I did.

Some consider this the first win in the Superbike class by a Japanese bike. It was made even more

rewarding by the fact that, at Pocono, Baldwin always seemed to have the upper hand. Exciting racing, hard work.

It was my only win that season, but my consistent placings were enough to earn my second national championship. Thanks, in large part, to Pierre Des Roches and his midnight flog. Godspeed Pierre.

(Linked Braking System) is designed to have exactly this effect. (When you apply the front brake, the rear brake is automatically applied in moderation, and vice versa.)

The key to the rear brake is to learn its sensitivity. If you stab the rear brake at just 20–30 mph, you can slide the rear wheel sideways 2–3 feet. Imagine what it will do if you lock it up at 60 mph! When the rear wheel is rolling, the brake is performing its duty—it's in control. When it's locked up, it's out of control. You need to recognize the dividing line.

How often do I apply the rear brake? At race speeds, I use it almost every corner. Most racers do. Consider the fact that Australian Mick Doohan, a five-time world GP champion, once broke his leg so badly that even after it healed he couldn't operate the rear brake. But the rear brake was so critical to him, he had a special thumb lever installed on the left handlebar to enable its use. Do you think he would have gone to this length if the rear brake wasn't important?

However, never use the rear brake when leaned over. As soon as you're off vertical, even a little bit, get off the rear brake.

Foot position is also critical. Most levers have adjustable reach. Position it so that your foot isn't hovering over the brake lever, toes in the air. Unlike the front brake, where you want your fingers to rest on the lever for instantaneous response, you don't want the rear brake to be this accessible. (In CLASS, I ask my instructors to look for people with their feet poised over the rear brake lever.) It's an invitation to crash. In a pinch, you want your hand to move before your foot. A lot of people do the reverse, which may be due to conditioning from driving an automobile.

DEALING WITH OBSTACLES

How should you slow down when you encounter surface irregularities such as gravel and sand, especially in a corner? First of all, the secret is to *set a speed that's within the limits of your ability.* If you encounter sand and try to put the brakes on at 80–90 mph, you'll get hurt. If you're going 20–30 mph, you can survive.

In general, if you stay off the rear brake, there's a good chance you'll come through these situations. Relax. Even if you get into a little slide, try not to let it faze you. A slide is nothing compared to the consequences of panicking, sitting up, and possibly drifting into the other lane. In so many cases, it is a panicked reaction to marginal circumstances that causes a rider to crash.

I'm always painting scenarios in my mind. Once, while entering a blind right-hander, I was doing just that. Sure enough, when I came around the corner, there was a huge truck in the middle of the road. Fortunately I could cope with it, because I'd managed my speed, set up properly for the corner, and was mentally prepared to react to such a situation.

It's helpful to imagine the worst possible scenarios. If you're ready, you'll manage. If you're not, the results could be very scary.

When it comes to dealing with sudden obstacles, some people feel it's better to "lay it down" as a means to avoid contact. Bad idea. I have too much of a can-do attitude when it comes to avoidance. I prefer to believe that I have the ability—borne of practice—to escape these situations unscathed.

In 2001 I had a 90 mph getoff at a CLASS session. Someone hit me. I did my best to manage the situation, applying the brakes right up to the tire barrier on the side of the track. By the time I crashed I had scrubbed off a lot of speed. My injuries would have been much worse if I hadn't done this. There was no way I was going to just "lay it down." I managed the situation as long as I could.

When faced with these situations, some people think, "I can't make it." In contrast, I'm very strong-willed about being able to pull it out. I say, "I can do this!" Most times I've won—a couple of times I've lost. But I'm convinced it's better to try to save it.

BRAKING IN CORNERS

In general, you should get most of your braking done in an upright position, where traction is greatest. However, sometimes you'll need to brake in corners, and sometimes you'll need to continue your braking into the turn. For racers, it's critical. For the average rider, it's something to at least be familiar with. Think of it this way: If your life depended on applying the brakes in mid-corner—for instance, if you encountered an

A NOTE ABOUT ABS

What about ABS (anti-lock braking systems), such as those fitted to some BMWs and a few other machines? ABS is very effective in building confidence, especially for someone who's scared of locking up the wheels. ABS gives you the confidence to approach this point, because you know the system won't allow a skid to occur.

I'm also an advocate of Honda's LBS (Linked Braking System). With it, I find I'm using far more rear brake, because it reduces the chance of locking up the rear wheel. (With this system, application of the rear brake also applies the front in moderation.) Basically, LBS desensitizes the rear brake.

In general, most manufacturers have reduced the size of the rear disc. You just don't need truckloads of braking power back there. It will only get you into trouble.

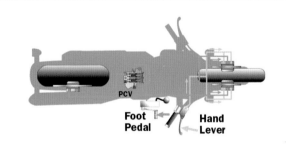

BMW's ABS (top) and Honda's LBS (bottom) are a tremendous asset to many riders, helping to prevent the wheels from locking up under hard braking. (Image courtesy BMW)

WHY RIDE THE TRACK?

AN INSIDER'S VIEW

Track riding makes you less likely to get into stupid accidents on the street. You have the focus, confidence, and control to avoid mistakes. In short, you know you can do it!

Joe Kerr is a longtime CLASS student who works hard to be a better rider. He is also a good friend, and has done graphic design work for CLASS and this book. Here he talks about the value of having attended dozens of CLASS sessions.

If you're predominantly a street rider, why would you ever want to go to the track or do something like CLASS? I've participated in almost 100 CLASSes, which is probably some kind of record. I also ride thousands of street miles every year. I'm always trying to improve my skills, and I think the track is one of the best places to do that.

On the track, you realize that your bike is capable of more than you believed possible. You are among instructors who look so comfortable doing things that make you nervous that it makes you think you can do it, too.

Many techniques take lots of practice to get right. This can be done on the street, but there is nothing like the track for honing these skills in an environment where you can really concentrate. You can focus on execution and let the speed follow naturally (which it does!).

I am always trying to improve my skills and there is nothing like the track for honing your skills in an environment where you can really concentrate. You can focus on execution, and then let the speed follow naturally. (Ian Donald Photography)

When speed increases you have to improve your ability to handle it. For example, no matter how many times you see Reg demonstrate the roll-on-roll-off throttle management technique, you find that you tend to "dump" the brakes at speed. It seems like there isn't time to do it any other way! But when you're going fast is exactly when smoothness really counts. An uncontrolled front brake release lets the compressed forks rebound and unsettle the bike—just what you don't want when entering a corner at speed.

It takes more than one session to really develop your skills. For example, you're told that to downshift you should keep your rpms up, execute quickly, and re-engage the clutch smoothly. You are told to make a downshift so quickly that the engine doesn't have time to lose rpms. It took me 11 CLASSes to get this right! I was long past the "chirping" tire problem, but after that it became effortless and really fun. So it's a constant process of increasing your skills, which increases your speed, which requires increasing your skills more, and so on.

All of this is supplemented with classroom instruction to emphasize and expand on the techniques. CLASS, like many schools, alternates track sessions with chalk talks.

All this training and experience makes you less likely to get into stupid accidents on the street. Accidents can still happen, of course. But now you have the focus, confidence, and control to avoid stupid mistakes. You are less likely to panic in an *I'm-not-gonna-make it* corner because of what you've learned on the track. You trust your tires because you know they've been through worse than this. You know how to use your entire body to make the bike turn. In short, you know you can do it!

Of course, all of this would be pretty stupid if it weren't fun! One reason people come back to the track again and again is because the experience and the people are so enjoyable. It's a great way to learn!

animal or other hazard—you need to have experienced it and not be scared by it.

How do you do it? Obviously, you can't just lean over at 45 degrees and slam the brakes on. This is an area where a good feel for your brakes and exceptional smoothness and finesse are essential for control. Most racers combine smooth front brake action with a sufficient quantity of engine braking to get the job done. Champions such as Miguel Duhamel and Nicky Hayden frequently "bring the rear wheel around" by overusing the engine's braking ability. They rev the engine, downshift two to three times, and lock up the rear wheel momentarily by feathering the clutch in and out.

This is where "trail braking" comes into play, which involves releasing the front brake as smoothly as you applied it. In other words, apply the throttle to accelerate out of the turn at the same time you're trailing the front brake off. Try practicing this movement in the garage prior to using it on the road or track. Once learned, trail braking will make the bike more manageable as you come back on the gas. The important thing is to manage these inputs subtly, because of the reduced traction while you're leaned over in a turn.

PRACTICE, PRACTICE, PRACTICE!

Maximum braking can't be learned in the milliseconds before an incident. It's something you need to plan for and put into practice. If you just wait for something to happen, it could be the last thing you ever do. You need to practice, *especially* when you feel you don't need it. The pros practice a lot, and you should, too.

How do you practice braking? You need a good imagination. Choose your place carefully. Parking lots can do the trick, but I prefer a real road that's free of traffic. I just let my imagination run and create scenarios: What if a car pulled out here? What if I encountered a patch of gravel?

Ensure that there's no following traffic, and imagine a braking point. Use a smooth, progressive application of the brakes to bring yourself to a stop as quickly as possible. Try using the same braking point over again to see if you can shorten the stopping distance. Experiment with just the front, then just the rear, and a combination.

I recommend that you encounter the limits of your braking regularly. If the rear locks up momentarily, you'll be able to get away with it. With the front, you'll hear a telltale howling noise as the tire approaches the limits of traction. Become attuned to this, but don't push it too hard—once the front locks up, you'll crash. It's a fine line. Know your limits, and operate within them.

4

THROTTLE MANAGEMENT

THE SECRET TO CONTROL

The term "throttle management" is a very deliberate one. Notice that I don't just say "acceleration." The word management implies forethought and control. How you manage the throttle has a profound effect on the chassis, suspension action, shifting, and cornering. In fact, it has as much effect as anything you can do on the motorcycle. The more thought you put into throttle management, the easier the bike is to control. *(Ian Donald Photography)*

roblem is, most people's approach to the throttle has nothing to do with management. They just want to whack it open or snap it shut. This can get you into a lot of trouble—especially with today's more powerful bikes.

Good throttle management can help you achieve better cornering lines, settle and stabilize your suspension, and help get you out of a hazardous situation. The potential dividends are huge—and so is the potential fun factor.

BENEFITS OF THROTTLE MANAGEMENT. *No matter what size bike you ride, and whether you're in a 100 mph sweeper or going to the corner store, the throttle is your guidance mechanism, affecting everything from suspension action to cornering line. (Photo courtesy American Honda Motor Co., Inc.)*

THE MAGIC OF RPMS

You've heard me say it before, but it bears repeating: *rpms are your friend.* This is one of the basic corollaries of throttle management, and it will pay dividends that you won't believe.

For the sake of instruction, let's look at how *not* to do it. Say you're in a corner at about 2,000 rpm. Here's what's happening with the dynamics of the bike: First, when you try to accelerate in mid-corner, the bike simply won't respond. The

engine is not in its power range. Second, the bike will not hold the desirable smooth line. Third, suspension action will tend to be unresponsive because it's near the bottom of its travel. Because the bike is "squatting" in this way, ground clearance will be reduced. Weight distribution is also altered, with an inordinate amount on the front and not enough on the rear.

Now let's look at how things are changed with ample rpms. First, you have power at your command for proper corner entry and exit speeds and anything you might encounter mid-corner. Next, by simply rolling the throttle on or off, you can widen or tighten your line in minute increments.

Keeping on the gas in the proper rpm range also lifts the bike slightly, putting it in the middle of its suspension range and increasing ground clearance. This occurs because the application of torque to the drive train (chain or shaft) causes the rear end to rise. Lastly, weight is distributed

evenly between the front and rear tires, for optimum traction. I bet you didn't know that rpms could do all that!

Whether you are riding a 500cc or a 1000cc bike, and whether you are running an errand, doing a 500-mile day, or riding on the track, the throttle is your guidance mechanism. It affects everything from cornering line, to suspension activity, to weight bias—and of course, to speed.

What does it mean to use ample rpms? With a modern four-cylinder, I tend to run between 6,000 and 8,000 on the street for normal riding. On the track, and for spirited riding on a twisty road, I use 8,000–12,000 rpm. For a pushrod twin such as a BMW, I recommend using 4,000–6,000 rpm, and for a Ducati V-twin, it's 6,000–8,000 rpm.

BEGIN AT THE BEGINNING: HOW TO GRIP THE THROTTLE

To grip the throttle for optimum control, I recommend you let the first and second fingers "float" over the front brake lever, and wrap the third and fourth fingers around the grip. This works well for most people, but it isn't etched in stone—your hand or grip size may dictate a variation.

Orient your hand on the grip in a way that allows quick changes. On most modern bikes, you need only a quarter-turn of the throttle to take the engine through its ideal rev range. (Older bikes may require a bigger fistful—or two.)

When in the middle of this range, and while sitting comfortably in the saddle, your wrist should be relatively straight. You shouldn't have to pick your wrist up excessively, or point your fingers down. Use only enough grip pressure to prevent slippage. Relax, but be firm.

Don't allow your bike to develop slop in the throttle cable, which can make your throttle management jerky. On most bikes it just takes a couple of small wrenches to remove the play at the adjustment barrel where it exits the twistgrip. You want just a fraction of freeplay.

After making this adjustment, be sure to twist the handlebar from side to side with the engine at idle to ensure there's no rise in rpms. If this occurs, the cable is constricted somewhere—a potentially dangerous situation.

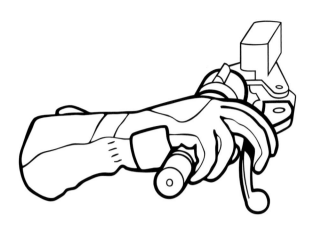

HOW TO GRIP THE THROTTLE FOR OPTIMUM CONTROL.
Rest the first and second fingers on the brake, and wrap the third and fourth around the grip.

THROTTLE MANAGEMENT AND CORNERING

Did you know that throttle management offers directional control in a corner? It's as simple as this: *Close the throttle to tighten your line (come into the inside of the corner), and roll on the throttle to push yourself to the outside.*

How does this work? Rolling off the throttle tends to compress the front suspension, reduce fork rake (quickening steering), and induce lean angle. Applying more throttle tends to arrest lean angle and straighten the bike slightly. Both of these changes affect your line in the corner.

Most people don't realize they can "steer" with the throttle. And it's not just for racers. It works on any type of motorcycle—cruiser or sportbike—and in any corner.

With the right rpms, and using fine throttle increments, this will enable you to corner smoothly at 70–100-plus mph. Obviously, at these speeds, control is critical. Don't snap the throttle shut or whack it open. We're talking about throttle "management," remember?

DOWNHILL CORNERS, TOO!

People ask me, "How can I use high rpms to negotiate a downhill corner? Won't I go too fast and run off the road?"

The answer is no! And the best proof I can think of is the legendary Corkscrew at Laguna Seca Raceway in California. This piece of track

ANATOMY OF A CRASH

I can hardly remember the first four or five years of my street riding, because I wasn't even thinking. I was just riding—out of control. All this changed abruptly one day in 1965.

At the time we used to race on an old airfield track at Cotati, north of San Francisco. As with many venues back then, it was never meant to be a racetrack. The pavement was very rough, with plenty of potholes, grass tufts coming up through seams, and no safety measures to speak of. This was normal for the day.

I was running second in the 250cc race, riding a single-cylinder Greeves Silverstone—a model affectionately known as the "Gravestone." I was chasing my perennial challenger, the Japanese rider Haru Koshino, who was riding the highly tuned and fast Suzuki 125 10-speed twin. My Greeves had potential, but little chance of staying with the factory bike—despite the displacement advantage. I was over my head from the start.

But who can tell a racer he doesn't have a chance? With two laps to go, I had fought my way to second place. It is at this point that time slows for me. I see myself entering a left-hander very quickly. As I tilt the bike in abruptly, the expansion chamber touches down. Predictably, the bike launches me into a highside. In an instant, I am airborne.

What happens next is lost to me, but is later related by bystanders. I am lying in the tall grass surrounding the racetrack, inert and lifeless.

Someone watching from the airport tower summons help. An Army medic arrives and pulls my tongue out of my throat to keep me from suffocating. I am transported to the hospital, incoherent. The only thing I remember is telling the ambulance driver, "You're my friend! You're Ernie!" Ernie Caesar was my sidecar passenger in those days. I was really out of it.

The next thing I remember is a nurse is cutting off my leathers. "No!" I tell her. My thoughts are not yet focused on my injuries, but on saving the expensive, borrowed suit. Typical racer!

Eventually, I learn the full extent of my injuries: a double compound fracture, three broken ribs, a broken clavicle, and a skull fracture which

I've just got to stop doing these suspension checks while riding! Ouch. Racers talk about "finding the edge." Well, I've found it many times in my career—and gone over to the other side on more than a few occasions. The important thing is to learn from the experience. (Photo courtesy Reg Pridmore)

Coming up through the ranks in the '60s I used to compete on 125s and 250s. I won a lot of races on this Bultaco 125, but it cost me a lot of skin. It revved to 12,000 rpm, but would also seize in a heartbeat, sending me head over heels for a hard landing! But racing it was great fun. (Photo courtesy Reg Pridmore)

causes me to bleed from the ear. My foot angles down off the table at an unnatural angle. My face is scraped and angry looking, thanks to the minimalist, open-face helmet I used back then. In short, I am a mess.

I stay in the hospital seven days. When I am released, I have a cast up to my crotch. Stainless steel stitches and Threadall (large pieces of steel threaded rod) have been used to knit my bones together. (A year and a half later, as a fitting memento to my crash, I use the Threadall as an oil tank mounting bolt for my kneeler sidecar!)

My wife, who is in England on vacation, knows nothing of my accident. Friends take me to the Los Angeles airport to meet her. "Don't be shocked," they tell her as I am wheeled out from behind a barrier at the airport. "Reg has had a little mishap." Little, indeed.

It is a year before I am riding again. Ironically, on my first solo ride, at the same track, I slide off in the same corner. All I can think is, "Please don't let my leg be broken again!" Fortunately it is a lowside this time, and I am fine. Damn that corner!

But something changed that day in 1965, and remains changed to this day. My recuperation provided plenty of time to think. Through it all, I became determined to have a better plan. I knew I could ride, and had the results to prove it. But I needed a better way of doing business. That better way involved lots of *planning, control, and smoothness.*

As I replayed the crash in my mind, all I could think of was that I had been delivering a bad message to the bike. My inputs were abrupt. After that, I started exerting better control over my bike, my mechanical preparation,

and everything about my racing and riding. Even more important, I developed an attitude of lifelong learning and improvement. Motorcycling, I realized, was something I could be better at but never completely master. No one ever can.

People sometimes ask me whether I thought of quitting after that horrific crash. The truth is, I never considered it. Racing meant too much to me then, as riding still does now. But after that day in 1965, something did change, and remains changed.

Believe me, you don't need to have the same experience to undergo a transformation in your attitude and your riding. Use mine instead. I give it to you freely, without the steel wire, the Threadall, or the body cast.

DID YOU KNOW THAT THROTTLE MANAGEMENT OFFERS DIRECTIONAL CONTROL IN A CORNER? It's as simple as this: Close the throttle to tighten your line (come into the inside of the corner), and roll on the throttle to push yourself to the outside. *(Ian Donald Photography)*

goes left, then right, then left again in quick succession, while losing the equivalent height of a three-story building. It can be frightening (but fun). It also illustrates how much control you can have at speed while going downhill. It instills a lot of confidence to discover that you can control a corner like this with the throttle "on." Low gear (first or second, depending on the motorcycle) will hold you back nicely and still give you the acceleration you're looking for on the exit.

On most bikes, first gear through the Cork-screw will have the motor working close to max-imum rpms. What about it? You're not going to hurt the bike. In fact, most modern bikes will happily take you to redline—at which point they'll shut off due to an electronic rev limiter. Whether on the road or track, don't be afraid to use maximum rpms if that's what it takes to ne-gotiate a downhill corner or give you the control you need.

THROTTLE MANAGEMENT AND SUSPENSION

Throttle management is closely linked to suspen-sion action. You want to keep the suspension "ac-tive" through a corner. This means it's in the middle of its travel, primed and ready to do business. I think of the bike as a boat that's leaving a wake through a corner, rising slightly under acceleration.

For a moment, imagine the reverse: you're in fourth gear, rolling off the throttle through a corner. The suspension is relaxed and asleep. The bike—like a decelerating boat—is sinking slightly, reducing ground clearance and increasing the like-lihood that you'll touch hard parts. Control is re-duced. It's a potentially devastating situation.

Don't corner with the suspension asleep. Keep it active and awake by using high rpms.

THROTTLE MANAGEMENT AND DOWNSHIFTING

Throttle management is critical for smooth downshifts. The secret is to maintain the correct rpm—one that makes engine speed match rear wheel speed. You need to bring these two things into harmony. Here's how:

1. Blip the throttle: If you've ever been to a race or watched one on TV, you're familiar with this one. Racers "blip" the throttle quickly and

ROLL ON THROTTLE

RAISES AND LEVELS BIKE FOR CORNERING CLEARANCE

THROTTLE MANAGEMENT IS CLOSELY LINKED TO SUSPENSION ACTION. *You want to keep the sus-pension "active" through a corner. This means it's in the middle of its travel, primed and ready to do business.*

smoothly prior to each downshift. Raising the rpms in this way gives the engine time to settle into the proper range by the time they've performed their clutch and shift action. It brings engine and rear wheel speeds back into harmony.

2. Keep the throttle where it's at: Another method is to simply maintain the same rpm—hold the throttle open and perform the downshift and clutch action with such lightning speed that the engine doesn't have time to fall out of synch with the rear wheel.

Say I'm on the track, coming into a 150-plus mph corner, and I want to go from sixth to fifth. I'll just leave the throttle right where it is and drop it into gear. I'm turning perhaps 11,000 rpm at this point, which is perfect. I just leave it right there.

CORKSCREW. *At Laguna Seca Raceway the corkscrew goes left, then right, then left again in quick succession, while losing the equivalent height of a three-story building. It can be frightening (but fun). It also illustrates how much control you can have at speed while going downhill. (Ian Donald Photography)*

Both of these methods take practice and sensitivity—that's the *art* of throttle management.

THROTTLE MANAGEMENT AND UPSHIFTING

Anytime you're going up through the gears, the magic words are: *Don't procrastinate.* In other words, don't be so deliberate in your shifts that you allow the rpms to drop off. This can cause the back end to do terrible things—at the least, a little chirp, and at the worst, a big slide. *Make your upshifts quickly.*

It helps to visualize what's happening in the gearbox—what's driving the motorcycle. The transmission is engaged via "dogs"—metal protrusions on the individual gears. To imagine this, take both hands, fold your fingers at 90 degrees, and interlock them. When these dogs are fully engaged, it's pretty hard to separate them (short of breakage). This is what drives the motorcycle forward.

To disengage them, you need to provide some relief via the clutch and the throttle. If you don't encourage this separation, they just won't come apart. By pulling in the clutch momentarily and easing off the throttle, you release the tension, and allow the dogs to separate and re-engage. When people say, "The bike jumped out of gear," what they mean is the dogs didn't engage solidly or they were worn and not holding well enough.

To ensure engagement, when you back off the throttle for just a fraction to make your upshift, keep your foot under the shifter and maintain slight pressure while releasing the clutch lever until you know the gear is fully engaged.

You can also upshift without the clutch. I do it often—especially on the track. You need to relieve a little tension (you can't do it with power fully on). In the blink of an eye, back off the throttle, make your gear selection, and get back on the throttle.

USING THE THROTTLE TO GET OUT OF A BAD SITUATION

You might not think that using high rpms would be synonymous with safety—but it is. Good throttle management provides a crucial margin of safety for you (and your passenger), especially when riding in town. By using a lower gear and keeping the rpms up, you have enough engine braking at your disposal to take care of most of life's little surprises, by merely rolling off the throttle.

Even a variation of a few hundred rpms can alter your speed significantly when the engine is operating in its ideal power band. Low rpms do not provide sufficient engine braking, or the ability to vary engine braking in fine increments.

There are also instances when a burst of power is just what you need. If you're running at

6,000 rpm, you can frequently rocket out of a bad situation, because the engine is in its power band and ready to respond. To prove this, you need only look at the horsepower graphs that accompany most magazine motorcycle tests. Horsepower rises exponentially in the upper reaches of the rpm range. But if you're at 2,000 rpm, you're stuck. The engine won't give you the same response.

BREAKING TRACTION

What would you do if the back end broke traction in a corner and "stepped out?" Most people would snap the throttle shut. It's a natural reaction. Unfortunately, it's also the worst thing you can do.

Here's another golden rule: *When the back end breaks free in a corner or under acceleration, try to maintain the same rpms until things stabilize.*

People look at me like I'm crazy when I say this—or they think I'm boasting. I'm not. When you snap the throttle shut, chances are that the back end will hook up and regain traction too quickly, leading to the most dreaded crash of all: the highside. The bike pops straight up, ejecting the rider like a piece of toast. Not a good thing!

I've had the back end step out more times than I can remember, and I've always fared best by maintaining rpms. Any racer will tell you the same thing. This is just as valid on the street when you encounter that small oil patch or pebbles in mid corner. Stay on the gas.

Unfortunately, it's not something you can practice on the street (or want to). All you can do is condition yourself mentally. Tell yourself, time and time again, *I will maintain rpms.* Rehearse the scenario on your regular rides. It's worth practicing, because the real thing can be scary and have dire consequences—if you react emotionally and make the wrong choice.

The throttle has so much to offer—if you'll make the effort to discover what it can do. It makes the bike more active, transforming it into something that's alive, and provides a tremendous measure of control and safety. And it will give you the biggest kick of your life.

THROTTLE DRILL

Here's a throttle management drill that will help assess your smoothness. I used this drill a lot to help teach my son, Jason. Try it on a straight, isolated road (no traffic if possible). Try making very short shifts from second through fourth and back down without significantly changing your road speed. Stay between 40 and 50 mph.

There are two ways to approach this. One method is to not move your throttle hand—just pull the clutch in about a third of its travel and go up and down through the gears. The other method is to maintain your rpms as you upshift, but to blip the throttle slightly as you come down through the gears.

This drill will really help you assess your shifting and whether it's jerky. You need to coordinate the throttle and clutch, and shift in one instantaneous motion. The key is to monitor the throttle—any variance will make the bike lurch or drag. The drill will also help you evaluate whether you are "dumping" the clutch.

It's a family affair: Two successful racers, Jason and Reg Pridmore, during a 1997 CLASS school.
(Photo courtesy Reg Pridmore)

5

BODY STEERING

A FULL-BODY APPROACH

Body steering is one of my strongest-held positions, and the thing perhaps most responsible for my success as a racer and instructor. It's also a huge part of my CLASS instructional schools. Simply put, body steering is using deliberate weight shifts and pressure on the footpegs and tank to promote smooth, relaxed cornering—and to reduce the required pressure on the handlebar. It's really that straightforward—you don't need Newton's equations or a physics lesson to grasp it. (Ian Donald Photography)

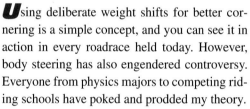

SAME CORNER, TWO DIFFERENT STYLES. *The rider in the photo above is staying centered on the bike. The CLASS instructor in the photo to the right is using pronounced body steering, with smooth, deliberate weight shifts and pressure on the footpegs and tank to get around the corner. Experiment to find out what works for you, moving off the saddle in small increments, increasing your commitment as you feel more confident and comfortable. (Ian Donald Photography)*

Using deliberate weight shifts for better cornering is a simple concept, and you can see it in action in every roadrace held today. However, body steering has also engendered controversy. Everyone from physics majors to competing riding schools have poked and prodded my theory.

So you need to believe me when I tell you: it works. I know this is true, my instructors know it, and thousands of CLASS graduates know it and have experienced its benefits.

One of the all-time greats of modern roadracing, Kenny Roberts, was once ridiculed for what were viewed as exaggerated and unnecessary body movements ("hanging off"). Three world championships later, no one was laughing anymore. Mick Doohan and Freddie Spencer (see sidebar on page 74) are other world champions who have extolled the virtues of using full-body input for effective cornering. It can work for you, too.

WHAT IS BODY STEERING?

Remember when you were a kid, and one of your parents pushed you off on your bike, and you felt balance come into play for the first time? If you swerved one way, you counteracted by leaning in one direction; if you swerved the other way, you leaned the other direction. It was totally intuitive and natural.

You may not have realized it at the time, but your input occurred through the pedals, the seat, and the handlebar, all at once, in a completely natural way. You never went through an analysis of gyroscopic stability or consciously said to yourself, "I need to apply a corrective action to the handlebar now." You just balanced.

This is body steering in its simplest form. But how does it work? A motorcycle (or bicycle) can turn only by leaning toward the center of the turn. At the same time, the front wheel must be steered slightly toward the direction of the turn. For a left turn, it will be pointed slightly to the left; for a right turn, slightly to the right. When these two things are done together—the lean and pointing the front wheel—the bike will begin to change direction. The angle of lean and the steering angle of the front wheel will have values that allow gravity and centrifugal forces to balance exactly for the speed you are traveling. Fortunately, we never

The most obvious example of body steering is riding a bicycle no handed. It's possible to follow a remarkably complex and curvy path on a bicycle without ever touching the handlebar. This is done completely by shifting body weight.

There is another way to get a motorcycle to begin its turn. You can steer the front tire *away* from the turn momentarily, so the bottom of the bike moves toward the outside of the turn, thereby making the top of the bike lean the other way. This is called "countersteering"—the rider steers the front wheel momentarily away from the turn, then into the turn. Another way of saying this is that you push on the left side of the handlebar to go left, and on the right side to go right. This technique works and it's fine to have it in your arsenal. But as we'll see in the rest of this chapter, body steering has enormous advantages in fostering a smooth, fast riding style. Why not try it?

RELAX!

If you've come this far in the book, you know that I like things to come naturally. I'm always seeking ways to eliminate tension. When your input comes from the whole body—body steering—you're reducing tension on your arms. You should have so little tension in your upper body that you can

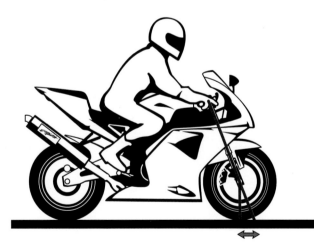

MOTORCYCLES HAVE A TENDENCY TO "SELF STEER" IN CORNERS. *That is, when the motorcycle leans left, the front wheel tends to turn left. This is due to gyroscopic forces, as well as something known as "trail"—the fact that the front tire contact patch "trails" the steering axis (shown by the blue arrow).*

have to think about the mathematical balance of these forces. If you lean over too far, the turn becomes sharper and the higher centrifugal force pushes the bike back upright; if you are not leaned over enough, the turn will not be tight and gravity will naturally pull you into a greater lean angle.

But how do you get a bike to begin its turn? Suppose you are traveling in a straight line. If you want to turn left, it is very natural—very intuitive—to move your body to the left. You can think of the motorcycle as an extension of your body and you want it to follow you to the left. If you want to go left, move your body to the left. This changes the center of gravity of your body—it has moved to the left, causing the bike to begin leaning left.

From here the motorcycle's front-end geometry causes the bike to "self steer"—that is, when the bike leans left, the front wheel steers left. This is due primarily to "trail"—the fact that the front tire contact patch "trails" the point at which the steering axis contacts the road. The net effect: you turn left.

AN INSIDER'S VIEW

TED HOLMAN: THE LIFE OF A CLASS INSTRUCTOR

Many riders wonder, "What is it like riding on the country's best tracks and teaching CLASS?" I can tell you that it's tremendous fun—but also serious work.

Somehow I find myself in the enviable position of being a longtime CLASS instructor. Like most of us at CLASS, I have a "real" job and don't teach to support myself. I do it because I enjoy it, and because I love to see the transformation that riders undergo during the course of the day.

A lot of street riders wouldn't normally think of spending a day at the track. Some are intimidated, or perhaps self-conscious about the fact that their bikes are not the newest and hottest models. Then there are my favorites, the ones who know everything they need to already. To all these riders, from Gold Wingers to MV Augusta owners, I promise you will realize these benefits:

- Improved smoothness on the throttle, brakes, shifting, and cornering
- Better control
- Increased speed
- Increased confidence

Many riders wonder: "What's it like riding on the country's best tracks and teaching CLASS?" I can tell you that it's tremendous fun—but also serious work.

Before traveling to CLASS, I do the same thing that most students do: I prepare my bike for the rigors of track use, inspecting it with a fine tooth comb, checking suspension settings, oils, cables, fastener tightness, and installing new tires. Meanwhile, Reg has already arrived at the track with his tractor-trailer full of bikes and equipment all prepared for the day.

The night before the school is always great. This is when I join some of my closest friends—my fellow instructors—and we enjoy a great restaurant meal. I could bore you with the juvenile behavior that has caused many a bus boy grief, but am sworn to secrecy. Let's just say that Reg isn't immune to this behavior—but he does tip well!

The following morning Reg is punctual and serious about preparing for the arrival of students. He has great pride in his organization. As instructors, it's our job to make this system flow as seamlessly as is possible. While others help register students, I perform tech inspections, ensuring that students' bikes and protective gear are ready for the day. It's always comforting to see the attention and detail most bikes have been given before we ever see them.

Next Reg assembles students in the classroom and delivers his opening remarks. This includes rules (no passing on the inside, no looking behind, no tailgating), guidelines for getting on and off the track safely, as well as common signals and communication. Meanwhile, we suit up and take a slow ride around. My approach is to view the track as though I've never been there before.

Then we line up in the hot pit lane ready for the A group—the advanced riders that have done a school at this venue before. They circulate with an instructor in the lead. The B group heads out with Reg to find a safe spot to watch our groups at different corners, demonstrating the "Pridmore Line": entering at mid-track, apex, and back to mid-track.

Next we take the B group for the same ride—small groups following an instructor. Some of these riders are apprehensive about riding on the track and so we take it very easy for the first few laps. It really takes a leap of faith for new students to begin to trust the track and their tires. I keep an eye on my mirrors to make sure everyone is within their comfort zone. The idea is to show new students where the track goes and where we want them to position themselves as they circulate later in the morning on their own.

After we have done these guided tours with both groups, we start alternating sessions: When the A group is on the track, the B group is in the classroom, and vice versa. Reg handles the classroom sessions the first half of the day, and we circulate with the

groups. Once in a while a student will pick up the pace a little too quickly and one of us will signal them to pull over into the hot pit lane for a little discussion. Normally this little get-together is enough to put that demon back in its box.

As the day progresses most students want to experiment on their own, implementing what they've learned in the classroom, while others approach us with questions. This is the part Reg stresses over and over: If you want help, grab an instructor and get it. There shall be no unanswered questions!

At lunch we offer a braking drill (see page 48) for B riders and anyone else who is interested. Recent CLASSes have also offered the opportunity to view videotapes of students, taken during the morning using one of the CLASS camera bikes.

After lunch things usually change gears. Most of the riders have developed confidence, and some need to be reminded of the consequences of riding over their heads. I pull them over and deliver these remarks in as gentle a manner as possible. On occasion I'll pass a rider and tap the back of my saddle, which is the sign to follow me for a little instruction on the correct line.

Do CLASS instructors get to have fun? Of course. Late in the day one or two of us will ride together at 8/10 speed, bar to bar, apex to apex, enjoying the skills that we have developed under Reg after all these years. It's a magical moment, but we also need to exercise restraint and focus on the reason we're here—to help students. If

Do CLASS instructors get to have fun? Of course. Late in the day one or two of us will ride together at 8/10 speed, bar to bar, apex to apex, enjoying the skills that we have developed under Reg after all these years. It's a magical moment! (Photos courtesy Reg Pridmore)

Reg sees us playing too hard, he pins our ears back!

By the end of the day we are totally exhausted but happy and full of congratulations for the students, who are invariably totally pumped about their day at CLASS. Each successful student is given a certificate of completion, to the applause of all the instructors and their fellow students.

Next is the task of packing up 15 bikes and the CLASS equipment. Finally, we assemble for dinner, which is a wonderful opportunity to reflect on the day and another successful school. We're usually pretty whipped, but anxious to do it all again.

BODY STEERING, PHASE ONE: *Imagine a line extending down the center of the bike, through the front tire, the headlight, and the windscreen. Body steering involves maintaining a position that is left of this centerline to go left, and right of this centerline to go right.*

BODY STEERING, PHASE TWO: *Incorporate the lower body into your cornering efforts. For a left turn, at the same time that you are moving the top half of your body across the centerline, apply pressure to the left peg using the ball of your left foot. Additionally, press your right knee against the tank.*

literally "flap your wings"—move your elbows up and down with total ease. Do this as a reminder to release tension in your upper body.

Why is this important? Tension causes over-reaction and eventually leads to crashing. Therefore eliminating it can literally help save your life. But that's just part of it. Reducing tension also enhances your riding enjoyment.

I'm always looking for experiences to be pleasurable, whether this involves riding a motorcycle, flying an airplane, or doing any other activity. In motorcycling, body steering is one of the things that will make it so. Try it and you'll see. Here's how:

BODY STEERING: PHASE ONE

Let's approach this in increments. To start, imagine a line extending down the center of the bike, through the front tire, the headlight, and the windscreen. Body steering involves maintaining a position that is left of this centerline to go left, and right of this centerline to go right.

Initially, accomplish this change by moving the top half of your body past the centerline—*especially* your head. Keep your butt stationary. In a left turn, some people put their left shoulder off to one side, but keep their head on the right. That's not what I want to see. You need to be looking over your left wrist.

Try this in the garage, statically, before going out on the street. Sit on your bike, relax the top half of your body, bend your elbows, and move across the centerline. Don't slide out of the seat (yet). This is the time to critique yourself without any rolling speed. Then, after practicing left and right statically in the garage, try it on a road at a moderate speed (35–45 mph). Do this in an area with little traffic.

You should find that you can make the bike go where you want without forcibly wrenching on the handlebar.

BODY STEERING: PHASE TWO

Phase two incorporates the lower body into your cornering efforts. For a left turn, at the same time that you are moving the top half of your body across the centerline, apply pressure to the left footpeg using the ball of your left foot. Additionally, press your right knee against the tank. I'm not talking about a violent effort here—these are

Body steering is all about putting yourself into a mental state of becoming "one" with your motorcycle—a flexible rider-machine combination. Instead of using just your arms to steer, you use your entire body. (Ian Donald Photography)

FULL BODY INPUTS

A LESSON FROM FREDDIE SPENCER

I had to find ways to conserve my energy and strength, and in doing so discovered that there were multiple ways to affect how the motorcycle steered and transitioned.

The year I won both the 250cc and 500cc championships, I had to find ways to conserve my energy and strength when running two 50-minute GPs back-to-back, and in doing so discovered that there were multiple ways to affect how the motorcycle steered and transitioned. If a rider relies entirely on countersteering, he or she must use muscle at a place where you need feel. In order for the motorcycle to transition through the corner using only countersteering, the rider must use a firm grip. This not only becomes physically tiring when done repeatedly, but also works to upset the chassis if done abruptly. I prefer not to muscle the handlebar.

Peg weighting is another method of steering that I teach. If you think of a motorcycle as a big gyroscope, at speed that gyro wants to continue moving in a straight line. You've got gears turning, pistons, wheels, and brakes...multiple moving parts that make turning the motorcycle all the more difficult. However, the footpegs are set low and act as an inside axle of the gyro, where a rider can maneuver his or her weight and use considerable leverage and pressure to affect how that gyro reacts.

One other method I recommend is using the outside knee against the fuel tank. This leads to a tightening of the torso muscles, which in turn allows the rider to take the weight off the arms. Why is this important? Because anything that helps alleviate a tense death grip on the handlebar will help the rider receive better feedback from the chassis and tires. And relaxed arms and hands are the direct instruments to have smooth throttle, brake, and clutch control.

One of the reasons I use such a diverse methodology when teaching students how to most efficiently steer their motorcycles is because a rider will use different techniques depending on the situation. On the racetrack, a rider can hang off the bike and use body and peg weighting more than on the street. During street riding, more importance may be placed on countersteering and brake/throttle application. But the important thing is to understand how all of these inputs can be best utilized to help maneuver the bike.

Freddie Spencer, three-time world champion, teaches his techniques at Freddie Spencer's High Performance Riding School. (Kevin Wing Photography)

very gentle movements. Try to be smooth with all of your transitions. If you find yourself having to white-knuckle the handlebar, then you aren't committing your weight enough on the tank and peg to lean the bike over. Make this weight shift in a smooth, relaxed fashion. Your arms should be bent. Remember, body steering is a means to reduce (but not completely eliminate) pressure on the bar.

Next, try it on the right side. Move the top half of your body right across the bike's centerline, placing your head almost over your right wrist. Keep your butt firmly planted in the saddle, and use the ball of your foot to apply pressure to the peg—a little at first, as you progress. Don't stamp on it.

BODY STEERING: PHASE THREE

Now that you've established a good foundation for your body steering technique, you can be a little more aggressive and start moving the cheek of your bum off the saddle, toward the desired corner (right for right-hand turns, left for left-handers). Again, try this first statically, with the bike on the stand in your garage.

I recommend visualizing a pivot point on the saddle, just behind the tank. Pivot your lower body around this point to produce the desired weight shift. For track riding, apply a little talcum powder to the saddle to help keep your leathers from dragging on the seat surface.

A word of caution as you enter this phase: It requires special sensitivity. Anytime you move yourself off center, you're increasing the time it will take to recover if the bike begins to slide. These movements *add* to your safety in the sense that moving more mass to the inside will enable you to keep the bike slightly more upright and enable you to explore the meat of the tire. But if the bike *does* begin to slide, your recovery time is decreased when your weight is committed in this way. It's a tradeoff.

Consequently, don't rush into this phase. Try it a little bit at a time, moving off the saddle in small increments, increasing your commitment as you feel more confident and comfortable.

BODY STEERING: PHASE FOUR

This is the final phase. It's more applicable to the racer, or the person who wants the utmost from

BODY STEERING, PHASE THREE: *Now that you've established a good foundation for your body steering technique, start moving the cheek of your bum off the saddle, toward the desired corner (right for right-hand turns, left for lefthanders). Visualize a "pivot point" on the saddle, just behind the tank. Pivot your lower body around this point to produce the desired weight shift.*

BODY STEERING, PHASE FOUR: *This involves "hanging off." When you are hanging off, your butt is almost completely off the saddle. Your main contact point is your outside knee, dug firmly into the tank. Your heels are dug into the footpeg hangers and your knee slider is on the ground, aiding stability*

DAYTONA 1976

Ironically, against the backdrop of all my racing successes, the event some people remember most was one that I lost: the 1000cc Superbike Production race in Daytona, Florida, in 1976. The photo finish makes its way into magazines even today, and for me, the story is retold with annoying regularity.

Every racer wants to win Daytona—it's a rite of passage for anyone intent on reaching the highest echelons of the sport (at least here in America). I was no different in this regard, and was eager to add a win in Florida to my racing resume. But it was not to be.

Daytona '76 was the culmination of a long campaign for me. I first went to the high banks in '71, on a Norton (Commando engine in a Manx frame). As would happen too many times in my career, this outing turned into a pitched battle with the "tech inspectors." I had installed an extra-large tank to help limit pit stops, but the inspectors would have none of it, citing some obscure regulation. I dutifully installed another tank, only to be cited again after parading through the very long tech line for a second time—in this instance for a non-standard front brake. I was ready to get physical with the inspector at that point, but my good friend George Kerker, of Kerker Exhaust fame, warned me off. So ended my first foray to Daytona, not a time in my racing life that prods me to like the "Big D."

I also returned to Daytona in '73 and '74, riding BMWs prepared by famed tuner Udo Gietl. Those were great races and furnished fonder memories, with the likes of Cook, Gary Fisher, Steve McLaughlin, Yvon Duhamel, and Wes Cooley circulating in close quarters.

In '76 I was riding the highly tuned BMW R90S. Much of the race was spent dicing with the usual cast of characters: my teammates McLaughlin and Fisher on BMWs, and Cook on the Ducati. Fisher retired with gearbox problems (he was a gorilla with transmissions), so it was down to me and McLaughlin on the final laps. Coming off the banking, I had significantly gapped him, and by the time I came onto the

Steve McLaughlin and I battle it out on almost identical BMW R90S Superbikes. Steve and I had great camaraderie as well as a fierce rivalry—the latter never more evident than at Daytona in 1976. (Photo courtesy Reg Pridmore)

home straight, I had six to eight bike lengths. *Great,* I thought. *I've got him. My first Daytona win!* (A racer should never utter those words.)

So often at Daytona, if you are in first position coming into the home straight, you need to do a lot of dodging to keep a following rider from drafting past. I thought my lead was enough that I didn't need to do that. Bad mistake. Steve managed to get in my draft after all, and at the finish, the photo told the tale: I had been beaten by less than half a wheel.

I was disappointed to say the least. When you lose by three or four bike lengths, that's one thing. *But a few inches . . . .* It's almost too painful to contemplate.

In retrospect, it was a good year for me. I won nationals at Laguna Seca and Riverside, California, which helped produce the first of my three championships. But those final seconds at Daytona resonate in memory to this day. It would be 21 years before the Pridmore name was vindicated on the high banks when my son Jason won the Daytona 750 Supersport race in 1997.

I had significantly gapped Steve McLaughlin at the end of the final lap at Daytona in '76, but he managed to get in my draft. At the finish, the photo told the tale: I had been beaten by less than half a wheel—one of my greatest racing disappointments. (Photos courtesy Reg Pridmore)

Always look through the corner and up the track—don't fixate on the area just in front of you. (Ian Donald Photography)

the motorcycle on the track. It means you're willing to give it your all to be better than the people you're running with. Many recreational and sportriders will never reach this phase, and that's fine.

Put simply, phase four involves hanging off. It's an extension of phase three, when you began to move your bum off the centerline. When you are hanging off, your butt is almost completely off the saddle. Your main contact point is your outside knee, dug firmly into the tank. Your heels are dug into the footpeg hangers and your knee slider is on the ground, aiding stability.

How far are you willing to take this? Hanging off requires a lot of thought and practice. You need to understand the other phases completely before attempting this. The techniques for hanging off are highly individual. One of the most remarkable is that of five-time 500cc world champion Mick Doohan. In photos taken from the outside of the corner, his body is barely visible—all you can see is the top of his helmet (if that!), the lower half of his leg, and his arm dragging over the tank. Full-body commitment!

This requires a superb sense of balance. Most of us will never get close to this level of commitment.

QUICK CHANGES

Does body steering work for quick changes in direction, such as when suddenly encountering roadkill or a pothole? Yes! I used to ride the dirt a lot, and I did trials competitions in England. I learned so much from off-road riding. One of the things I realized was that you can steer with your legs to get around obstacles. My good friend Danny Walker, who runs the American Supercamp dirt track schools, teaches these same techniques.

When I encounter sudden adversity, I use my body more than anything else, initiating the change in direction with my legs and feet. It works. Those that knock it usually can't do it—or don't want to make the required effort.

WHAT ABOUT COUNTERSTEERING?

Proponents of countersteering focus on applying pressure to the handlebar to initiate a turn. The idea of pressing down on the inside handlebar is reinforced by the resulting motion of the

YOUR UPPER BODY. *When your input comes from the whole body—body steering—you're reducing tension on your arms. You should have so little tension in your upper body that you can literally "flap your wings"—move your elbows up and down with total ease.*

WHEN YOU'RE READY. *Start to move the top half of your body across the bike's centerline, placing your head almost over your right wrist. As you're doing so, look through the turn.*

bike as the inside drops and heels into the turn. Usually it's summed up in this way: Push on the left handlebar to go left, or on the right handlebar to go right.

LAGUNA SECA 1976

My win at Laguna in 1976—en route to my first national championship—was a career highlight. It's also known for a widely circulated, almost surreal photograph of teammate Steve McLaughlin's BMW being launched, riderless and totally inverted, at 100 mph. This photo was so spectacular that it made it big time into the *Los Angeles Times* and many other publications of the day.

What the papers didn't say was that while McLaughlin and his bike were imitating a cruise missile, I was up the road and on my way to a very satisfying victory.

The race had an inauspicious beginning for me. I was never a great starter, and this trait required me to methodically work my way through the field during the course of the race. By applying steady pressure, I'd force my competitors to make mistakes, and so advance by attrition and careful planning. I'm sure other racers found this highly annoying, but it worked. Competition was

My win at Laguna in 1976 is known for a widely circulated, almost surreal photograph of teammate Steve McLaughlin's BMW being launched, upside down, at 100 mph. Meanwhile, I was up the road and on my way to a very satisfying victory. (Photos courtesy Reg Pridmore)

very close back then. On any day, there were a lot of guys who could win. I figured it might as well be me.

On this day the formula was working to perfection, as Gary Fisher retired with an imploded transmission, and I gradually worked my way past the others. Before long, McLaughlin was the only rider still in front of me. I lined him up for an outside pass in the short straightaway that was known as Turns 8 and 9 (now changed to Turns 10 and 11). I took the lead, and kissed my little leprechaun buddy goodbye.

Unbeknownst to me, moments later, McLaughlin suffered his spectacular crash, etched forever into film and history (thanks to the brilliance of photographer Mush Emmons).

At the time, I knew nothing about it. My practice has always been to never look back during a race. It can only slow you down, so what's the point? Consequently, I didn't know McLaughlin had crashed until the next lap when I saw him standing there, disconsolate, by the side of the track. (Fortunately, in contrast to his thoroughly wadded bike, McLaughlin was fine, and gave me the famous British "V" for victory sign.)

It was a tremendous feeling circulating the track that day with a victory flag—that was the picture that *should* have made the papers the next day, but crash and burn always sells better!

DOES COUNTERSTEERING WORK?

Of course it does. You can get a motorcycle to follow the desired path exclusively by applying pressure to the handlebars, with no other body movement. Is it the best way? Not in my experience, and not in the experience of most racers I know. Try riding a tight figure eight with your feet off the pegs. It's not too easy, is it?

No one racing at the highest levels today could do so without moving their bodies over their motorcycles and applying differential weighting to the pegs and tank. You need only view a videotape of a race to see simple and unequivocal proof of this, as riders make pronounced movements over the top of their bikes.

You can, of course, *complete* a lap of the track sitting stiffly on the bike and using only handlebar input. But no rider in the modern era of roadracing has ever won a championship without additional chassis input in the form of body English, or as I call it, body steering.

Body steering puts me in control. I move my body where I want to go and the motorcycle follows. Even at an easier pace where I'm sitting in the center of the seat I'm still using my legs to

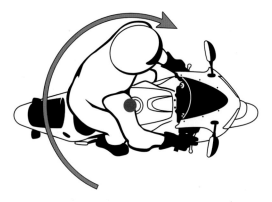

weight the pegs to help me steer. The mental process of countersteering puts the motorcycle in the lead: I have to push it where I want it to go and I follow along. For the motorcycle to become an extension of my own body, I have to put my full body into it. The resulting feeling is exhilarating.

People love to talk in absolutes. They say, "don't do this" and "don't do that." That's never been my way. Body steering has worked for me throughout my career, and for thousands of CLASS students. Why not see if it works for you?

TOP. *How much do you want to hang off? The choice is yours. Just keep in mind that anytime you move yourself off center, you're increasing the time it will take to recover if the bike begins to slide. (Ian Donald Photography)*

LEFT. *Visualize a pivot point on the saddle, just behind the tank. Pivot your lower body around this point to produce the desired weight shift.*

6

CORRECT CORNERING

THE BEST WAY 'ROUND A BEND

In the motorcycling community, the subject of cornering lines carries all the emotion of a political debate. Should you enter the turn from the outside, or the inside? Should you use an "early apex" or a "late apex?" Is it quicker to enter fast and exit slow, or enter slow and exit fast? In this chapter I'll answer these questions by supplying some simple, proven cornering techniques. *(Kevin Wing Photography)*

SHOULD YOU ENTER A TURN FROM THE OUTSIDE, OR THE INSIDE? *Should you use an "early apex" or a "late apex?" Is it quicker to enter fast and exit slow, or enter slow and exit fast? Cornering can be a real art form! (Ian Donald Photography)*

I'm a racer and have spent a good part of my life teaching riders how to ride quickly. So people are sometimes surprised to learn that one of my most common pieces of advice is: slow down. The most important first step for cornering is to set your bike, your body, and your speed before entering the turn. If you've set your speed correctly it will be easier to follow the correct line. And on the road if you follow the correct line, you'll be in a better position to avoid oncoming vehicles and other hazards.

How do you set your speed correctly? There is no formula for this. You need to be constantly evaluating road conditions and visibility through the corner. Your judgment will be based on the last several turns, as well as what you see in front of you. In general, set your speed in a way that will enable you to accelerate through the corner, as described in the chapter on throttle management.

On the track, the variables are minimal. There's no oncoming traffic and you know which way the next turn goes, and you should plan accordingly. But in either case, if you're going too fast initially, the natural reaction is to panic, apply the brakes, and deviate from the desired line.

This is also a case of "going slower to go faster." Setting your speed correctly for the turn will enable you to accelerate smoothly through to the exit. In other words, by being conservative on entry speed, your overall time through the corner will be reduced. If you go in too fast and are forced to brake, you'll squander the available traction, disrupt your timing . . . or worse.

Many riders go into an unfamiliar turn too hot, only to discover it's a decreasing radius corner. Consequently, they completely cross the double yellow line on the exit for a right hander, or run off the road at the exit in a left hander. Some people won't slow down until they have the pants scared off them—especially when they're running hard with others. The riders who want to be as good as the other guys are the ones who get in trouble. I recommend that you set your own pace.

KEEP A TIGHT LINE

On the road for most right handers and on the track for most turns, I recommend that you keep a tight line. It's another one of my golden rules.

On the road, this means starting from the center of your lane, hitting the apex, and finishing out the corner. (The apex is the imaginary point on the path through the corner that is closest to the inside boundary of the turn.) In contrast, a wide line is one that uses the maximum amount of road available. For a right hander, the wide line involves going from the far left of your lane, to the apex, and back out to the far left of your lane—from double yellow to double yellow.

Granted, the arc of the tight line through a corner has a shorter radius than that of a line that extends from double yellow to double yellow, and so initially requires more traction for a given speed. But the benefits are worth it.

ON THE ROAD: RIGHT HANDERS

The tight line keeps you safe by maintaining ample distance between you and oncoming traffic. By entering a corner from the middle of your lane, you keep distance between you and vehicles in the opposing lane. This is especially important when these vehicles drift into your lane—as they so often do.

It gives you more maneuvering room on the other side of the corner. By entering in control and on a tight line, you have more choices upon exiting the corner. If the road allows it, you can accelerate hard. If you encounter road kill or a pothole, you'll have more maneuvering room than the person who is using the full road width, going from double yellow to double yellow. On left hand turns it's important to stay to the right portion of your lane until clear visibility can be had through the turn.

ON THE TRACK: RIGHT HANDERS OR LEFT HANDERS

The tight line is a defensive position relative to other riders. On the track, a tight line will prevent people from trying to pass you by running up your inside. It gives you more time for upright braking to get into the corner deeper. On a tight line, you begin your turn at a different angle and stay upright closer to the apex. While you're still upright, your brakes are more effective than when you're leaned over.

Riders who master a fast tight line on the track develop more skill to place the bike anywhere necessary in spirited track riding, competition, or on the street in emergency situations. Once you've established your entry point at the middle of your lane (or at mid-track), you should use the most gradual arc possible to get through the corner. For a given speed, a smooth, gradual turn requires less cornering force and lean angle. A gradual turn also uses up less of your available traction and provides more cornering clearance.

I've talked about the golden rule of tight lines for the track and for right handers on the road, but what about left handers? A blind left hand turn presents a different situation and is one of the only times I vary and run a wider line. I would widen my entry line in that case, move over to the right, to be sure that I'm as far away from oncoming traffic as practical. In either case on the road, be it right or left hander, if there is clear visibility through the turn, I have no problem with stepping up to the double yellow line.

COUNTERPOINT: STAYING WIDE

Many instructional programs advocate entering the corner at the widest possible point—for instance, just right of centerline for a right-hander on the

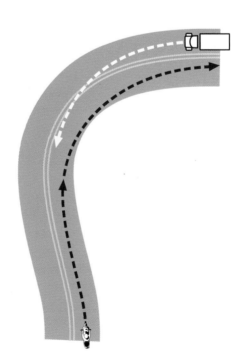

THE TIGHT LINE KEEPS YOU SAFE BY MAINTAINING AMPLE DISTANCE BETWEEN YOU AND ONCOMING TRAFFIC. *By entering a corner from the middle of your lane, you keep distance between you and vehicles in the opposing lane.*

A LEVEL HEAD

Do you keep a level head when you're riding? I mean this figuratively and literally. While you should always look through the corner toward the exit, your eyes should stay parallel to the road or track surface. Even when fully leaned over, keeping your eyes level will help your perception and keep you oriented in your surroundings. This means moving your head upright to the left for a right-hand turn, and vice versa.

Some people have a tendency to tilt their heads with their shoulders and bodies. This has an effect on your inner ear, and disturbs your equilibrium. It's detrimental to the accuracy of your lines and cornering inputs.

This rider shows a good, aggressive riding style. He's looking through the turn, his eyes are parallel to the track surface, and his body is off to the inside of the bike with his elbows bent and shoulders dropped. **(Photo courtesy Suzuki Motor Corporation)**

street. The theory is that this position produces the best visibility through the corner, enabling you to see what's coming on the other side.

I disagree with this approach for a number of reasons. A lot of accidents occur when the motorcyclist runs into oncoming traffic. The rider may be within his or her lane, but the automobile driver cuts the corner, crosses the centerline, and moves into the rider's path. If both vehicles are traveling at 50 mph, this makes a converging speed of 100 mph. In these circumstances, it will be nearly impossible to avoid a collision.

Common sense, and my own experience, tells me that my chances of survival are greater by staying away from a 5,000-pound vehicle bearing down in the opposite direction. This is why I advocate the tight line. Enter the corner in the center of your lane, or just right of center.

Many riders are intent on maintaining the highest cornering speed possible by using the maximum road width—going from double yellow to double yellow. Please tell me: Where is it written that you need to maintain 50–60 mph through turns at all times, and use all of the road? Sooner or later, riders who do this are bound to get hurt.

There's another problem with wide lines—they leave little room for maneuvering. Say you're on a big tourer such as a Honda Gold Wing with limited cornering clearance. If you're already on the double yellow and a car crosses into your lane, you won't be able to lean into the corner any further or you'll touch down hard parts. It's only a matter of time until you'll panic, sit up straight, and shoot into the opposing lane. Why would you want to risk that?

Tight lines save lives. My own experience has proven this many times. Personally, I want to survive and enjoy motorcycling for a long time. I don't want to flirt with SUVs in the oncoming lane. Those vehicles will hurt you badly if you are not close to the center of your lane at the corner entry.

EARLY VS. LATE APEX
A lot of riders talk about their preferences for an "early apex" or "late apex" (see diagrams on page 91). What does this mean? Basically, if we're talking about a right hander on the street,

an early apex line means you will come closest to the right road edge early in the turn, and finish wider (close to the centerline). A late apex line means you do the reverse: Enter the turn wide (close to centerline) and come closest to the right road edge later in the turn, near the exit.

For me, this question of early or late apex has more to do with setting your speed than any deliberate choice of line. I can't emphasize enough the importance of monitoring your speed when entering the corner. When you've established your speed correctly for the conditions, your line will largely resolve itself. Let's take a look at how this works:

The early apex. Most riders who use an early apex are simply carrying too much entry speed. This means that as they come into the corner, they can't get the bike leaned over sufficiently. For the racer who has the full track at his or her disposal—and who has the ability and confidence to lean the bike hard—this may not be a problem. Most racers can overcome an early apex, and it may even provide a passing opportunity. But for the street rider who carries this much speed into the corner, the tendency is to sit bolt upright on the corner exit, cross the opposing lane, or perhaps even go off the road edge. In other words, they can't get the bike leaned over enough to complete the turn. Disaster.

The preferred apex. A mid apex line—which keeps sufficient room between you and opposing traffic—is the natural byproduct of setting your speed correctly for the corner. You need to enter at a speed that will enable you to accelerate through the turn. Your judgment will be based on road conditions, visibility, and what you've experienced in the last several turns. (Err on the conservative side.) When your speed is set correctly, you'll find that you exit the corner under control and without flirting with the double yellow or oncoming traffic.

The late apex. A late apex also makes good sense and can keep you safe—as long as your entry is not too wide, you are in the correct gear, and have set your speed correctly beforehand. A late apex will give you the option of accelerating harder on the exit, without having to step up to

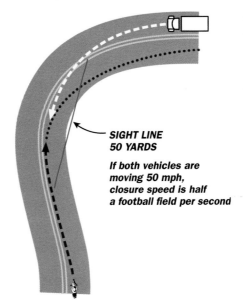

SIGHT LINE 50 YARDS

If both vehicles are moving 50 mph, closure speed is half a football field per second

THE WIDE LINE IS DANGEROUS. *My own experience tells me that my chances of survival are greater by staying away from a 5,000 pound vehicle bearing down in the opposite direction. This is why I advocate the tight line rather than the one shown here.*

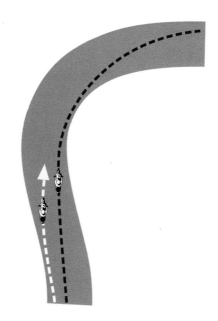

THE TIGHT LINE IS A DEFENSIVE POSITION RELATIVE TO OTHER RIDERS. *On the track, a tight line will prevent people from trying to pass you by running up your inside.*

the double yellow. A late apex is particularly suited to the track, where you want maximum corner speed and you know exactly what awaits you on the other side.

I've also found that late apexing is common among riders who use the so-called wide line. By using my tight line, and by setting your speed correctly, your path through the corner will evolve naturally.

RACES TO REMEMBER

BATTLE OF THE LEGENDS 1992–1997

In the 1990s—more than 10 years after my last race—a unique opportunity came my way: to compete in the company of some of the world's best racers from the '50s, '60s, '70s, and '80s—most of them my heroes.

This special race series, sponsored by the American Historic Racing Motorcycle Association and BMW of North America, was called the Battle of the Legends. The idea was to give the fans a glimpse of their heroes in a fun, informal format. To flatten the playing field and promote the sponsor's bikes, everyone was to ride identical late-model BMW twins, being of equal tune and performance. Events were to take place at Daytona Beach, Florida, Loudon, New Hampshire, Sears Point, California, and Lexington, Ohio.

At the time, this is an exciting prospect for me, since it means I will

be racing in the company of some of my heroes, including Dave Aldana, Don Emde, Dick Mann, Gary Nixon, Phil Read, Roger Reiman, Jay Springsteen, John Surtees, and many others.

For the first year or two of the series we ride 1000cc air-cooled twins, in a special white edition. Later, we graduate to the newer, 1100cc oil-cooled twins. While these bikes are portly and underpowered by today's sportbike standards, they are good track tools nonetheless. We run the motors right to the rev limiters in high gear on the banking at Daytona—an indicated 150 mph. I have a tremendous comfort level with the bikes, having raced BMWs extensively, and used them in CLASS in the mid '80s and early '90s.

Of course, the idea is to provide the fans with some good-natured

entertainment. But something curious happens when we all get on the track and the flag drops. Here come the race faces. Things get serious. After all, there is something irrepressible in a racer. You can't put a bunch of ex-national and world champions on a racetrack and expect them to be gentlemen. These guys want to win, and so do I.

Several incidents stand out in memory. One year, at Daytona, I find myself with a good line coming into the ballsy and difficult Turn 1. I go around the outside of several riders, including Nixon. However, in mid-turn, someone moves over on Nixon, who in turn moves over on me. Suddenly, I feel Nixon's right-hand cylinder head pressing down on my left shoulder. Thankfully, we get untangled and manage to stay upright. But later, I discover a

The Battle of the Legends provided a great opportunity to compete against some of the world's best racers, some of whom I had only read about. Here I am leading four-time AMA Grand National winner David Aldana. (Photo courtesy Rob Mitchell)

The Battle of the Legends brought out the racer in all of us. What was supposed to be a "show" was really a fairing-banging competition! Here, Gary Nixon is hot on my heels out of Turn 5 at Daytona. (Photo courtesy Don Bok)

burn mark on the shoulder of my leathers where we came into contact. Gentlemen, my arse!

One other year at Daytona I am leading Nixon and Jay Springsteen, nose to tail, coming into the chicane, when the rear end of my bike steps out in a heinous fashion. We were on the gas hard in a right-hander just before the exit of the chicane, when my rear wheel breaks loose and the back wheel seems to slide forever, and I feel sure that I am destined for a humongous and painful highside. In all my years of racing I don't remember ever having a slide like that. However, as is my practice, I stay on the throttle, and somehow, the rear end comes back into line. Major pucker factor—fresh underwear is the order of the day! I manage to cut

across the grass and miraculously find myself still in the lead. All I could think of is, "Thank you God!" During the post-race interview over the public address system, Nixon's first comment is: "Did you see that?" pointing to the chicane and the site of my little misadventure. Both he and Springsteen are veteran flat-trackers, but they agree that "Reg'o can flat track with us anytime!" I was very proud—not sure how I did it—but proud nonetheless.

Unfortunately, the series ended on a sad note. The Grand Finale took place in March '97 at Daytona. Roger Reiman, AMA Grand National Champion and three-time Daytona winner, crashed in the early morning practice. As always, we were riding in really close quarters, and unfortunately Roger was hit by a following

bike and never regained consciousness. Roger and I had become fast friends during the previous four years, and this event marked a sad ending to my time spent racing with one of America's greats.

Overall, it was a privilege to compete against such great riders, some of whom I had only read about. The racing at the front was always tight and exciting, and many times the first four across the line were within a wheel of each other. Great stuff! The races were also surrounded by some fun ancillary events, including banquets and marathon autograph sessions. For all of us, it was a great opportunity to revisit the glory days. The stories of those events—like all of us racers—keep getting better with age!

If you are disciplined enough to know your exact cornering line, and hit your markers every time, then you can begin to experiment with a second or third line. In a race, this provides a means to pass or outwit your competition. *(Ian Donald Photography)*

DECREASING RADIUS TURNS

A decreasing radius turn—one that becomes progressively sharper—is one of the greatest cornering challenges (see illustration on page 96). By its very nature, the decreasing radius turn offers little visibility of the road ahead.

Of course, as you've gathered by now, your most effective tactic occurs before even entering the corner, by using your engine and brakes if necessary, and setting your speed conservatively. A lot of riders have a tendency to push the speed and are no longer in a position of control when confronted with a decreasing radius turn. Setting your speed correctly will give you the margin to maneuver, use more lean angle, employ body steering techniques, or even use the brakes in mid-corner without breaking traction.

Nonetheless, the time will come when that corner just keeps wrapping around until you need to take action . . . now. The most important things are to focus on the task at hand—and stay off the rear brake! Too many riders, when faced wih a decreasing radius turn, look at what awaits them on the outside of the turn—such as oncoming traffic. They lose confidence, panic, and can no longer manage the situation.

What you need is more lean angle. One of the things that will pull you through is to look through the corner. This means swiveling your head—not just your eyes. Look as far up the road as practical, and the bike will follow. On bikes without a lot of clearance, leaning farther may not be an option, so you will need to be even more careful about getting into a turn like this too hot.

INCREASING RADIUS TURNS

Here's where the fun comes in. The increasing radius turn, which opens up more the deeper you go into it, offers the greatest margin of safety and the greatest opportunity for enjoyment.

Visibility in these turns is usually excellent. As a result, you can accelerate hard on the exit without undue drama, and use more of the roadway. In a broad, 60-degree left-hander with excellent visibility, you might even step up to the double yellow (the one exception to my tight line rule) if traffic is clear.

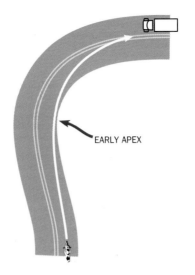

EARLY APEX

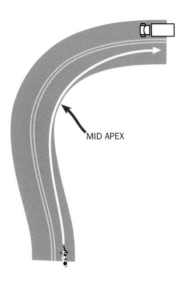

MID APEX

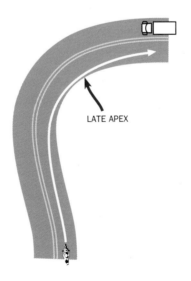

LATE APEX

EARLY APEX. *Most riders who use an early apex are simply carrying too much entry speed. For the street rider, the tendency is to sit bolt upright on the corner exit, cross the opposing lane, or perhaps even go off the road edge.*

MID-APEX. *This is the preferred line. It keeps sufficient room between you and opposing traffic, and is the natural byproduct of setting your speed correctly for the corner. When your speed is set correctly, you'll find that you exit the corner under control and without flirting with the double yellow or oncoming traffic.*

LATE APEX. *This line also makes good sense and can keep you safe as long as your entry is not too wide, you are in the correct gear, and have set your speed correctly. A late apex will give you the option of accelerating harder on the exit, without having to step up to the double yellow. It's suited to the track, where you want maximum corner speed and know exactly what awaits you on the other side.*

HOW YOU COMPLETE ONE TURN AFFECTS YOUR ENTRY INTO THE NEXT TURN.

If you swing wide on the exit of the first turn, you'll be in the incorrect entry position for the second turn. Overall, the tight line is what will provide the necessary margin of error and enable you to deal with any surprises.

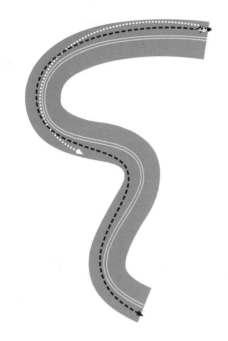

A SEQUENCE OF TURNS

Some of the most rewarding riding comprises a flowing series of turns, where the road surface is clean and you can see through far enough to have confidence as you lean into each corner.

But what happens when you throw in a decreasing radius turn, or encounter a little shale in the middle of an otherwise perfect sequence of corners? You need to be constantly evaluating the information coming your way. If the road is smooth and clean, you can run slightly higher speeds than you would otherwise. On the other hand, if the visibility is poor due to roadside vegetation or other obstacles, you'll want to back off. Consistently good visibility through the turns is what really makes riding safe and enjoyable.

Also, as every racer knows, how you complete one turn affects your entry into the next. For instance, let's say that a constant radius right-hander is followed by a decreasing radius left in rapid succession. If you swing wide on the exit of the first turn, you'll be in the incorrect entry position for the second turn. One mistake begets another. Overall, the tight line is what will provide the necessary margin of error and enable you to deal with any surprises.

Body steering is key to smoothly negotiating a series of turns. Every corner demands different inputs. Sometimes you don't have to get out of the saddle; for other turns, you may need to slide one cheek off the seat and apply a little pressure to the inside footpeg. For still sharper corners, you'll need to pull the bike over with your outside knee. The more comfortable you are using this range of inputs, the smoother, faster, and safer you'll be in a sequence of corners.

THE MID-CORNER CRISIS

I approach every corner, whether it's right or left, with the idea that something's waiting for me around the bend.

There is no limit to the things you might encounter around the next bend. There could be coolant in the road, blowing sand, or frost. You might get hit with a powerful wind gust as you crest a ridge or emerge from a tunnel. A friend of mine once rode over a palm frond, and it took the front end away. I once hit a small dog. Was I surprised? Yes and no. The fact was, I had made the decision about what to do long before, setting my priorities for on-coming traffic avoidance. I made up my mind that if it came down to hitting a dog or veering into oncoming traffic, I would hit the dog. So in a sense, I didn't have to make a split-second decision. The choice had already been made. I hit the dog and came through just fine (so did the dog).

People always ask me: You can do that? You can decide these things in advance? Of course you can! Every one of us can prepare to overcome a bad situation, whether it's a palm frond, bad weather, or just some dirt in the road. Sooner or later, these things are going to be thrown at you. Will you have planned ahead? Will you be up to the challenge? Those of us in California practice our earthquake preparedness. Since September 11, we prepare for terrorism. So tell me—why shouldn't you prepare for every eventuality on your motorcycle? It can save your life.

I sometimes joke that I ride with the idea that there's a dead horse around the corner. (I actually did find a dead horse in the road one day.) I never really let myself become totally relaxed (although there are times when I lighten up). I'm always thinking about the what-ifs. The road conditions are there to master, and they are a challenge. Your job is to deal with all of it and be ready.

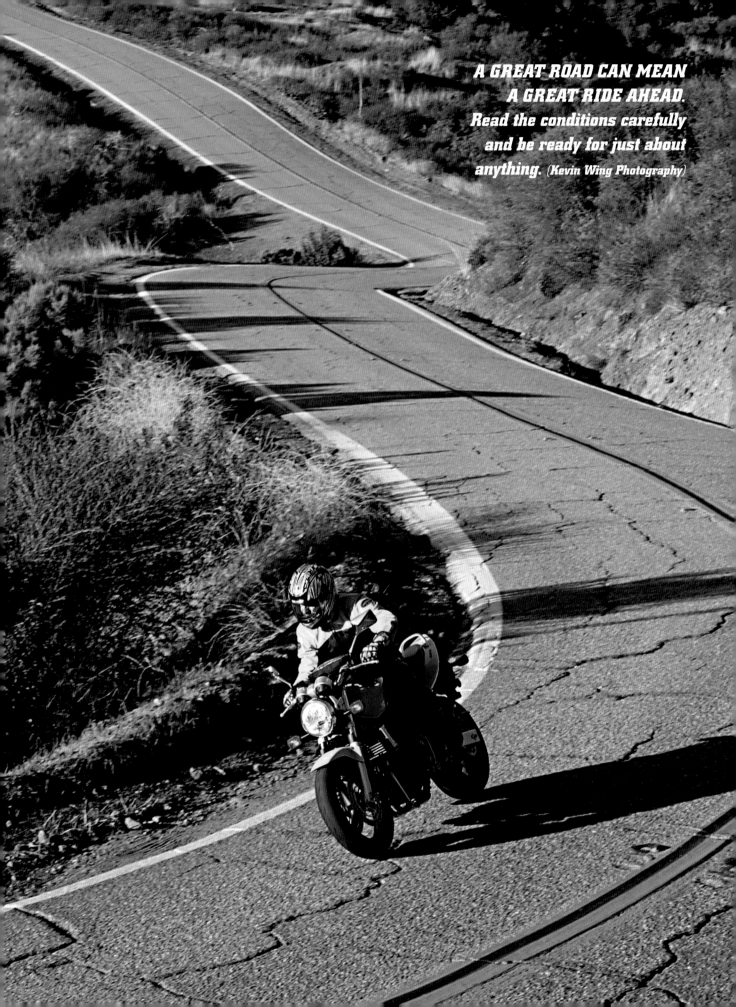

A GREAT ROAD CAN MEAN A GREAT RIDE AHEAD. Read the conditions carefully and be ready for just about anything. (Kevin Wing Photography)

THE CONNECTION BETWEEN MOTORCYCLING AND FLYING

There is an inescapable connection between planes and bikes. I fly, and I've known so many pilots who are also motorcyclists, that it can't just be a coincidence. Banking a plane into a gradual turn, performing a perfectly executed roll, or experiencing the Gs as you descend through the Corkscrew at Laguna Seca—these things go right to the pleasure center in your brain. Maybe there's a kind of genetic infatuation with acceleration and extreme lean angles. If so, I've got it bad.

My obsession started during World War II, growing up in Hornchurch, Essex, in England. I knew what a Spitfire was from the time I was four and got to see them in action. I didn't really comprehend what war was about—I was just fascinated with flying. How could it be possible to leave the earth and return at will? That thought nestled in my subconscious and remained there. Still does.

But as a practical matter, flying seemed unapproachable. I came from a modest background, and for a long time I never thought I would own a motorcycle—much less a plane. But in the late '70s, when I still owned RPM (Reg Pridmore Motorcycles), I became friends with a customer who flew and taught flying. He encouraged me to take up flying, and we struck up a barter arrangement—I taught him to be a better motorcyclist, and he taught me to fly. I took to it immediately. By '79—a year later—I had my license.

Since then my passion has only grown, and I've been lucky enough to fly a variety of planes, including a Spitfire Mark IV, a North American P-51 Mustang, and an F16. I even got to use the SR71 flight simulator at Edwards Air Force Base in '98. (To me the sleek, titanium SR71 is the most remarkable plane ever built.) Through it all, I've found tremendous similarities between flying and riding a high-performance motorcycle.

But the connection doesn't just involve pleasurable sensations. The best pilots and motorcyclists have a shared instinct for smoothness, control, and keeping a level head when it comes to understanding panic and self control. Believe me, I know.

One of the two planes I own is a '46 Globe Swift. I call it my hot rod—a beautiful, highly polished aluminum two-seater known for its performance and handling. The year is 2001. I am coming in for a landing when I discover that only two of the three green lights that indicate the status of my landing gear are illuminated. One wheel is still retracted. At this point, time begins to slow. I inform my passenger, carefully, of our situation.

I realize there are choices to be made, each one leading to another—each one critical. I issue a May Day over the radio. Someone on the ground with binoculars notifies me that, contrary to the indicator lights, the rear wheel is in fact down—at least partially. Good news. The fact that I am not getting a green light means that it's not locked in place. I will have to live with that.

A friend jumps in his plane to fly alongside and further confirm what is happening. Since I am faced with a dire situation, he recommends drastic action: ascend several thousand feet, put the plane in a steep dive, and then pull up as hard as possible. I do as he says, and await a result—anything. Suddenly, I hear something like a bowstring snap into place. *Twang*. It worked! Now I have three wheels down, and two greens. Not optimum, but better. This is turning out to be some ride. And we're not home yet. We decide to land.

Far below, on the airstrip, I see fire and emergency crews rolling, celebrity status I never wanted. Because I have no faith that the rear gear will hold (still no green light on final!), I keep it on the front two

wheels for as long as possible. Finally, I touch down in back and...it holds. We are safe. Ironically, as I turn and begin my taxi...whump—the back wheel collapses underneath us. No matter. We are back on terra firma, with virtually no damage!

What does this have to do with motorcycling? A lot. Even today, I continue to replay those moments in my mind—those choices. Each time we swing a leg over a motorcycle, we set a sequence in motion. Each choice has consequences, which in turn begets more choices. Sometimes, we find ourselves in a circumstance for which there is no logic or reason—and a choice can provide the exit door to safety.

The sum of all these choices has a name—it's called control. It is the

essence of this book, and the essence of motorcycling. Once you let your emotions take over, you're in trouble. You've relinquished control.

I don't believe in the slogan, "No Fear." It's good to have fear. Harnessed properly, fear can ensure control, as I found out that day.

There's also a feeling you get when you're doing it right, whether you're in a plane or on a bike. I fly very much by the seat of my pants—sometimes, simply for the rush that makes me tick. I can tell if the plane is slipping or sliding by the feel it gives me right down the middle of my spine. I try to ride motorcycles the same way, using smooth throttle and braking inputs to achieve a feeling of control and satisfaction.

I honestly believe there is a little bit of pilot in every motorcyclist, and vice versa. Both know that the combination of desire, understanding, and practice can pay big dividends—and maybe just save a life.

There is an inescapable connection between planes and bikes. I fly, and I've known so many pilots who are also motorcyclists, that it can't just be a coincidence. Here I am in my restored '46 Globe Swift. **(Photo courtesy Mike Terry)**

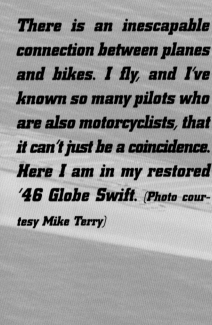

It's also crucial that you not fight the handlebar in these circumstances. Many riders, when confronted with a mid-corner surprise, tend to exert a death grip on the bar and move it forcefully. Such sudden movements can cause the front wheel to break loose and exacerbate the situation. My approach is just the opposite: relax and let the motorcycle do its job. Once, on Highway 138 near Lake Hughes, California, I came around the corner to discover a huge amount of shale and mud in the road. The only way I came through the loose stuff was by adopting a relaxed position on the bar. I hit one rock and that was it. Since my inputs were gradual and I was working with the bike rather than against it, I came through OK. Had I tensed and made abrupt handlebar movements, I feel sure I would have slid the front end out. Every once in a while you have to find out that you can hit things and not go down. This requires conditioning your mind.

CORNERING ON THE ROAD VS. THE TRACK

My keystones of good cornering—setting your speed and using the tight line—are just as valid on the track as they are on the street. But there are some differences.

The track is a known quantity. One of the many advantages of the track is that it doesn't change or throw surprises at you. For instance, we know that Turn 2 at Laguna Seca always goes left. On a road that you're not familiar with, all the principles change, particularly when it comes to setting your speed. If you're not aware of what's around the corner, slow down. On the street, I'm a bit of a wimp until given the "all-clear" (near perfect conditions and visibility).

The track provides more leeway when exiting the corner. In CLASS I recommend that students enter most turns from center track (the tight line). But on the exit, if necessary, you can accelerate right to the edge of the track. This is a luxury you don't have on the street, where you have SUVs bearing down from the opposite direction.

The track can be committed to memory. On the track you can strive for perfection. You can memorize exact shift and brake points (using the markers provided) and duplicate your line to within an inch or so on every lap.

The track provides a softer landing. In CLASS I give students all the tools and know-how they need to finish the day in an upright position. And most do. However, accidents happen. No crash is to be taken lightly, but at least on the track riders are spared the prospect of oncoming vehicles. The stakes are not as high as on the street.

A DECREASING RADIUS TURN. *In these situations your best tactic is to have set your speed conservatively, leaving a margin of error. One of the things that will pull you through is to look through the corner. Look as far up the road as practical, and the bike will follow. (Photo courtesy Yamaha Motor Co., Ltd.)*

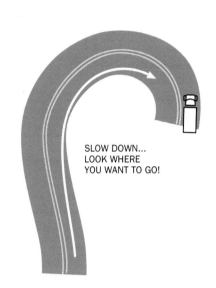

SLOW DOWN...
LOOK WHERE
YOU WANT TO GO!

FINAL THOUGHTS

It is more difficult to keep a tight corner entry line and keep your cornering speed up. It tightens the turning radius and requires more lean. But learning it also gives a rider more skill in the long run. Once you can master a tight line, you'll have more skill to put the bike where you want to in any situation. Where do the fast guys do their passing? On the inside—and they have to be able to get through quickly. Many fast riders and club racers come back and tell me how much better they've gotten by pulling their lines in—better braking, better passing underneath, higher finishing position.

So it takes more skill to keep a tight line and be fast. Years ago, my son Jason began helping out with CLASS and started riding at the track. As he grew up and got better and better at riding he used to say, "Dad, I can't do that—stay tight and still go fast." And at the track I would constantly go up the inside of him. He set his mind to it and before long he was closing the door on me and eventually trying to slip underneath me—I don't leave the door open too often! But he proved that the "can-do" attitude was all it took and Jason went on to become a very good professional racer and national champion.

At race speeds, you usually need to widen your line a bit, but this doesn't mean that you need to use the entire track entering the turn, and it doesn't mean you have to change your apex. Chances are as speed increases, you'll be beginning your turn earlier. But remember, if you leave the door open, somebody will go through. I still get around the track at a pretty good clip, and do it keeping a protective line. If you insist on a wider line than me, that's OK, but I'll go under you. So you'd better tighten up that line!

Remember: "slow down to go fast." It sounds strange, but changing old habits means replacing them with new ones and slowing down helps. Once you can master a new line or a new technique, the speed will build on a correct foundation. Get the technique right, get the line right first, then the speed will come.

LIFE SAVER

I have a cornering checklist that I drill into students at CLASS. It goes like this:

- Downshift
- Set your speed
- Enter on the tight line
- Look through the corner
- Accelerate through the turn, as early as you can

Does it work? Time and again, students tell me that it does—and in many instances, that it saved their lives. This account is typical of the letters I receive:

(Ian Donald Photography)

Many at the CLASS session I attended at Road Atlanta were grumbling about trying to keep a tight line around the course. I always keep an open mind when it comes to instruction and who am I to second-guess a multi-time AMA champion? I followed your instructions and learned to deal with it.

Soon after, a practical example of the necessity to keep a tight line was dramatically demonstrated to me during a four-day trip to the Blue Ridge Mountains in North Carolina. Prior to taking CLASS I was a notorious centerline rider, as I believed it gave me room to run into a corner faster and kept me away from the gravel that can be found on the pavement edges.

While riding with some friends, I was practicing the tight line and getting comfortable with the technique. I entered a blind right turn only to find a work truck well over the centerline in my lane. It was only because I was keeping the tight line that I did not become a grim statistic. I surely would have died that day if it had not been for your instruction. I thank you for the lessons I learned at your school!

Lloyd Horton
Atlanta, Georgia

7

STREET STRATEGIES

EFFECTIVE EVERYDAY TACTICS

In this chapter I'll give you valuable tools to survive in the urban jungle—things that have kept me safe for almost 50 years, and for hundreds of thousands of miles, in countries all over the world. Unlike some racers who elect not to ride on the street, I've always enjoyed road riding. I'm out there most weeks.

*B*efore we start, here's another one of my golden rules: *What works on the track also works on the street.* The cornerstones of good technique that I've been advocating throughout this book—things such as control, smoothness, and focus—are essential no matter where you ride. You need to take care of business the same way.

Of course, the speeds are different. You should never attempt to simulate track speeds on the street. But when it comes to the fundamentals and what the bike will and will not do, the same principles apply. So if you've come to this point in the book, you're already quite far down the road to being a better street rider.

CONCENTRATION: YOUR CONSTANT COMPANION

Many people think that mental concentration is only required on the track because the speeds are greater. But believe me, you need the same doses of concentration at 25 mph on the street that you need at 125 on the track. Even a casual run to the corner market requires extreme concentration. Statistics continue to show that most accidents happen within a short distance of home, and frequently within the first minutes of a ride. You

A BUSY INTERSECTION. *Stay extra alert and watch out for those racey or oblivious types that turn left in front of you. Also be aware of light jumpers—drivers who just have to make it through after the light has turned red. This rider is in an alert position—he's got his front brake covered, ready to use. His foot is back off the rear brake and his arms are relaxed, with his elbows bent and not locked.*

need to have a plan, be prepared, and be focused—no matter what the distance or duration of your ride.

Our public roads continue to become more dangerous, largely because people are complacent in their driving habits. You see this every day: motorists with mobile phones, focused on everything *but* driving their vehicles. As a motorcyclist, you can never be complacent. You need to think about every intersection, every stoplight, and every stop sign.

I honestly believe that at some subconscious level automobile drivers feel that they won't be hurt in a collision. Consequently, they're much less diligent than they should be—especially when it comes to motorcyclists. Given these feelings, they will pull right out in front of you and perhaps never even register in their minds that there's a motorcycle coming.

How do you improve your odds in these situations? By ensuring that your observations are where they should be. When I'm riding on the street, I simply will not let my concentration be broken. It's just not in my book. When I'm riding, it's intense—whether I'm going slow or fast. You need to conduct yourself the same way. At any moment, you may need to make a split-second decision. You'd better be ready.

CAN IT STILL BE FUN?

I've painted a pretty grim picture here. If you have to ride around on high alert, always wary of the other person and assuming the worst can happen at any moment, how can you still enjoy motorcycling? It's a matter of picking your places. If you know the road you can ride at a sporting pace. If you choose your points carefully, on a twisty road you know well, you can pull it off quite safely. You can build in fun by playing with acceleration and lean angle. You don't have to lose your sense of enjoyment just because of your heightened awareness, or because you're riding on public roads.

I don't recommend that you try to get your fun in town. According to accident studies, the vast majority of motorcycle accidents occur on city streets, with cars. When riding on surface streets, going from block to block and light to light, you should rarely leave first or second gear

or exceed 25–45 mph. You need to conduct yourself carefully in that environment. Leave the fun factor to open roads that you have feelings for and know well.

GO WITH A PLAN

I put a lot of emphasis on planning—whether I'm piloting my airplane, riding on the track, and especially riding on the street.

Planning takes many forms. We're all familiar with large-scale plans, like those you'd make for a trip. This type of plan might involve packing your bike, choosing a route, and determining where you'll stop for gas. There are smaller-scale plans such as: How will you approach this intersection? How will you execute this pass? What will you do if that SUV turns left in front of you?

But it doesn't stop there. For the competent motorcyclist, planning extends to the smallest moment in time such as: How will you execute this shift from second to third? How quickly will you roll on the throttle in this corner exit?

Even if I'm just going to the corner store, I still have a plan. I know where I'm going, how

I'm going to get there, and exactly where my focus needs to be. I execute every corner and shift deliberately. This type of awareness adds immeasurably to safety.

People ask me, "Why would you need to plan for a two-block trip?" I'll tell you why: Because you could die in two blocks. It's the same phenomenon with helmets. People say, "I'm just going a few blocks, why do I need a helmet?" Somehow, people don't think they need to implement safety measures or plan for a short ride. It's a tremendous fallacy, as statistics have shown.

The rest of the people on the road are not there to be nice to you, and they'll hurt you if you get sloppy. Don't give them the opportunity. Plan ahead.

PROJECT A CLEAN IMAGE

When I'm on my motorcycle, I project a clean image. This applies to the condition of my machine, and also to the way I conduct myself when I'm riding, particularly on the street. Most times I try to behave myself. I was a bit of a cowboy in my teens and I had some close calls. I took those

BE READY! *When I'm riding on the street, I simply will not let my concentration be broken. It's just not in my book. At any moment, I may need to make a split-second decision. I want to be ready!*

STREET RIDING

CRAIG HANSEN

Even the best instruction can't educate you about every potential danger. You need to be constantly examining the clues all around you, processing the information, and taking action.

Craig Hansen of Medford, Oregon, has been a CLASS instructor since 1995, and was a CLASS student for more than 10 years before that. He's been riding since age 20. "Early on I just got hooked on what Reg was teaching," says Hansen. "It was like the start of motorcycling for me—the beginning of a whole new era of excitement. And I'd ridden for 15 years already!" Hansen teaches at 10–15 schools a year, and his son, Mason, is also a CLASS instructor. That makes three generations of Hansen motorcyclists—Craig started Hansen's BMW/Triumph/Ducati/KTM in Medford with his father in 1972.

In the beginning I think a lot of students come to CLASS to learn how to go faster on the track. They don't always realize how useful those same skills are on the road. Obviously, the track is a more controlled environment. But body steering, throttle management, smoothness, and all the other skills emphasized in CLASS are important in both situations. With these skills in hand you can focus on whatever challenges are thrown at you and adjust the bike with confidence. The motorcycle becomes a part of you—a second limb.

I liken CLASS to training for an athletic event. Someone training to run a mile doesn't just train one mile at a time—they need to go beyond that and test themselves. Many motorcyclists are riding at 90 to 100 percent of their ability, with no room for error. CLASS provides an opportunity for riders to explore and expand their limits. Then when the inevitable occurs—such as a car pulling out from a side street—a trained rider is only using 70 percent of those skills.

You have to be so much more aware on the street now than you did 10 or 20 years ago. The roads are more crowded, and there are more distractions than ever. You must be more skilled and more aware than the other guy.

To me, street riding is a game of chess. At first glance, I'm just a pawn. I don't have the size and presence of a car or truck. But with my skills and savvy, I can still win the game. I have the power of a king or queen. Here are a few things I've learned:

DON'T GET COMPLACENT: At some point in every ride—whether it's a trip to the store or a 300-mile day—there comes a point where you say, "I'm almost home." At that point, *watch out*. I've trained myself so that the minute I say that, I adopt the attitude that the ride is actually just beginning. I pump myself up to a new level of awareness. Statistics have shown that so many accidents happen near home. That's when you really need to be defensive.

WATCH THE BLIND SPOTS: After an accident, most motorists will say they never saw the motorcyclist. The rider could be entirely in the right, but as the saying goes, they could be dead right. It's up to you to ride smart. On a multiple-lane road, never ride to the right/rear of a car. Similarly, don't float along next to someone—accelerate and pass, or slow and drop back where you'll be seen. Don't follow closely behind a truck because you are invisible to oncoming traffic. Someone in the opposing lane waiting to cross your lane into a side road will cut in behind the truck—and right into you. Also, when behind a line of traffic, move over to the centerline periodically to show your headlight to opposing traffic. When you see a line of traffic coming toward you, there is probably someone anxious to pass using your lane. Move to the right side of your lane for best visibility. Think about all the scenarios that could put you in a blind spot, and take action to use the whole lane to prevent them.

WHEN PASSING ISN'T PRUDENT: It can be incredibly frustrating to be stuck behind a slow car on a nice road. But if passing means that you'll endanger yourself or scare the hell out of the driver in front of you, I recommend that you just pull over. When riding in a group, we'll do this frequently. We stop,

yak for a while, and wait as long as we can. When we see another car coming from the rear, we get back on the road and enjoy the riding until we catch the slower traffic. Usually we get to our destination just as quickly, without putting ourselves at risk, and we have a lot more fun doing it.

BE A DETECTIVE: Even the best instruction can't educate you about every potential danger. You need to be constantly examining the clues all around you, processing the information, and taking action. For instance, if I'm commuting at 8 am, I go on high alert because I know people on the road at that hour are probably late to work for many reasons. Drivers are stressed because of the kids, alarm didn't work, dead battery, and on and on. The results are people running lights, improper lane changes, or road rage. I use the same level of caution at 5 pm, because people are tired and irritable from a stressful day at work.

Be aware of the businesses on the roads you travel. If I see someone exiting

A lot of students come to CLASS to learn how to go faster on the track. They don't always realize how useful those same skills are on the road. With these skills in hand you can focus on whatever challenges are thrown at you and adjust the bike with confidence. (Ian Donald Photography)

a bar, I exercise extra care for obvious reasons. In the vicinity of a hospital, I figure people might be in a rush, or are emotionally distraught because of a family illness. During sunrise or sunset, if the sun is not in my eyes, then it is in the eyes of oncoming drivers, and I know I'll be invisible to them. I've gathered a lot of this information from real-world incidents, or those that my customers have experienced. But the list never ends. You need to be thinking constantly and develop your own list of dangers.

HE MAY LOOK LIKE A DRAG RACER, BUT THIS RIDER HAS MENTALLY CONDITIONED HIMSELF TO BE AWARE OF CROSS TRAFFIC AS HE PULLS AWAY FROM THE STOP. *Take a quick look to the left and right before entering the intersection—watch for the light jumpers! If you have to wait a bit, keep one eye in your mirror with an escape route in mind, just in case a driver comes up hard and fast behind you.*

AT A STOP SIGN, MAKE EYE CONTACT WITH OPPOSING DRIVERS AND LOOK FOR SUBTLE HEAD MOVEMENTS. *Notice whether the front wheels are starting to turn, or if the hood lifts. Tune yourself in!*

as warning signs. After a while I realized it was wrong to play racer on the street. This was one of the reasons I went to the track—to see if I really had what it takes.

Now I'm older and wiser. I may rip in the right places at the right time, but I'm under control more now. The street is not the place to show off. I won't let myself get pulled into a racing

situation. I don't pull wheelies or annoy people with excessive noise. At a four-way stop, I tend to let the other guy go.

BE PREDICTABLE

We've already talked about the importance of discipline and focus in all your riding. On the street, these things translate to predictability for those around you. It means operating at or near the speed limit in town, avoiding rapid lane changes, stopping in a smooth and controlled fashion, and not cutting back in too close to a car you just passed.

Remember, motorcycles are capable of fantastic acceleration and braking—but motorists may not be expecting these rapid speed changes. They're more accustomed to the closing speeds and gradual movements of cars. You need to take this into account in your riding.

INTERSECTIONS

Statistically, more than half of motorcycle accidents and fatalities occur at intersections. The dangers come from every angle: cars pull out in front of you, turn across your path, run a light or stop sign, hit you from behind—and myriad other scenarios. Is there anything you can do to improve your odds in these situations?

For starters, remember that you have a plan. You would never try to navigate the Corkscrew at Laguna Seca Raceway without a plan; nor should you approach intersections without one.

What are the ingredients of an intersection plan? First, always be in a lower gear with the rpms up. Be ready on the brakes as you approach any turning and crossing situation. In particular, emphasize the *front* brake. In town, and for most of your riding, cover the front brake lever with two fingers, as discussed in Chapter 3.

Constantly run scenarios through your mind as you approach intersections. Try not to let anything surprise you. People will signal left and turn right; they will accelerate, pass you, and turn across your path; they will look you in the eye, smile, and pull out in front of you. This stuff happens all the time.

You can get mad about it, or you can be ready for it. Pretend that motorists are blind. (It's a fact that after an accident, many motorists say, "I never saw him!") Be ready for these things before they happen.

THE FOUR-WAY

At a four-way stop or signal, some motorists will use their turn signals—but many will not. For this reason you should never treat a green light like a drag race start. Hesitate that extra moment to be sure of where the other person is going.

Another reason to hesitate at a green light is that cross traffic will often run the red. If you take a flying start through the intersection, you could get T-boned (unfortunately, I've been there, done that!).

If it's a stop sign, make eye contact with opposing drivers and look for subtle head movements. Notice whether the front wheels are starting to turn, or if the hood lifts. Be attuned to these things.

THE DREADED LEFT-TURNING MOTORIST

In this situation you are going straight through an intersection and the opposing motorist turns left across your path. Statistically, these accidents account for a large percentage of motorcycling deaths. This scenario is the Bad One, and you need to prepare for it.

You legally have the right of way in such circumstances, but that's little solace—it won't do you much good from a hospital bed. I've seen people with their left turn signal on who look me straight in the eye—and then pull directly across my path. The fact is, they are thinking about work, home, dinner—anything but you. It helps to have your headlight on and wear bright clothing, but it's no guarantee of safety. Trust no one.

How do you improve your odds against the left-turning motorist? When approaching a busy intersection, slow a little, downshift, and cover the front brake. Hard braking is one of your best options. If necessary, you can also take evasive action such as turning to the left, away from the car. With this type of plan, you can greatly improve your chances of survival.

Again, look for signs such as head movements, front wheels starting to turn, or the hood starting to lift as the car begins to cross your path.

Lane position can also help make you more visible to left turners. Don't hide behind large vehicles or SUVs as you proceed through the

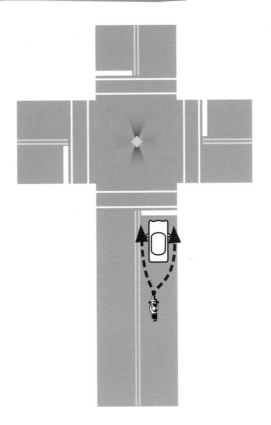

IF YOU'RE COMING TO A RED LIGHT, MOVE OVER TO THE RIGHT OR LEFT. *Don't sit on the bumper of the car in front—leave a bike length or two. These measures supply an escape route should a car threaten to hit you from behind.*

BAD PLACE TO BE. *This rider is asking for trouble. He's going straight, but oncoming left-turning traffic won't be able to see him, as he's blocked from their view by the pickup truck. It is best to stay back and left to remain visible to oncoming traffic.*

THE ULTIMATE RACING CHALLENGE

If you were to look at the history of the legendary Isle of Man TT and peruse a list of its most famous racers—you wouldn't find my name. The first time I went, my bike had problems before the start, and I never even got a chance to ride. Two other times I DNF'd. One year, 1971, I got a bronze finishing plaque, which I cherish. But there were never any podiums for me, or any newspaper headlines.

But in my mind's eye, my Isle of Man experiences are huge—among the most important of my career. For me, the legendary TT still stands out as the ultimate racing challenge. In this day of closed-circuit tracks, protective air fences, and generous runoff areas, the famed Mountain Course—with its narrow lanes and stone walls, seems improbable and extremely dangerous. Add to this the steadily increasing lap speeds—up to an average of 127 mph for solo and 112 for chairs, at last count—and you have a spectacle like no other. No racer or visitor can ever forget the Isle of Man, and almost all have the irrepressible desire to return again soon.

What makes this event so special? There are hardly any races held on public roads anymore, and this fact alone makes the IOM—a race held since 1907—completely unique and extremely demanding on man and machine. The natural beauty of the place is inspiring, with its pastures, sheep, old stone walls and buildings, beautiful little country lanes, and shorelines dotted with thousand-year-old castles. The weather, with its diabolical fog and rain, can make walking difficult, much less riding a motorcycle at ton-plus speeds. The TT stops for nothing and no one.

The place names along the 37-mile Mountain course are legendary in themselves, and evoke strong memories for me: Douglas, Quarterbridge, Bray Hill, Ballaugh, Ramsey, Gooseneck, Windy Corner, Creg ny Baa. Just as famous are the racers who mastered the course, including Geoff Duke, John Surtees, Giacomo Agostini, Phil Read, Jim Redman, and of course Mike Hailwood, who won 14 TTs in his career, and once even won three categories in a week. Later came the era of Joey Dunlop, who won a remarkable 26 TTs in his career.

Most people think it's nuts to want to push the envelope at such a place as the IOM but you have to be in awe of guys lapping at 120-plus mph with nothing but hay bales to protect them from phone poles and rock walls. There is a certain magic that draws a racer to that experience. You either shy away from it, or you have to do it. I had to do it. And even though I don't consider my performances to be stellar, the Island

For me, the Isle of Man is the ultimate racing challenge. Average speeds of more than 120 mph on the narrow roads make this a spectacle like no other. No racer or visitor can ever forget the experience. That is me with passenger Kenny Greene. (Photo courtesy Reg Pridmore)

Kenny and I at the Island in 1978. We were about half-way through the 37 mile course, making good time. Smooth teamwork was a big part of racing sidecars. Pilot and passenger are doing a little low flying in this photo!

(Photo courtesy Reg Pridmore)

is like nothing I've ever experienced.

Though I had been aware of the TT seemingly forever, my first trip there didn't occur until 1969. The adventure starts before you even get to the island. As if to prepare you for the rigors you are about to undergo, the ferry ride crosses a roiling Irish sea. Most of the passengers get sick—a sort of IOM initiation ritual.

I had tested my special Manx Triple (Kawasaki 500cc two-stroke in a Norton Manx frame) at Brands Hatch the week prior, only to finish 11th with clearance problems, which helped me decide not to run the bike at the Island. Instead, I used a loaned, street-legal 125cc BSA Bantam to make a sighting lap. The poor little bugger seized several times on my first circulation, and that was the quick and unspectacular end of my first Isle of Man experience. No matter—I was hooked.

In '71 I returned with my RGM Norton Commando sidecar outfit, with Ernie Caesar as passenger. We were able to finish 32nd out of 78 starters and earn a finishing plaque. We were also able to lap in practice

at over the magic ton—101 mph—fairly close to the winning sidecar speed of the day. In '78 and '79 I returned with a Yamaha TZ750 sidecar outfit, with Kenny Greene as my new IOM passenger. Both times we failed to finish.

It's not just the racing that makes the Isle of Man so memorable—it's the atmosphere. Thousands and thousands of bikes arrive for the TT each June, and a sort of mania grips the Island for two weeks. We always made a fun trip out of it, taking our families and doing touristy things, including a visit to the mountaintop Motorcycle Museum (only to discover a large poster of myself on the wall!). We rented two vans for the duration to carry our bikes and gear, which came in handy when the weather changed to rain.

It wasn't all seriousness, either. I remember a lot of time spent in the Douglas pubs and playing around when the demands of racing allowed for a free moment. We sometimes stayed outdoors playing Frisbee until we couldn't see anymore, which in Island time is about

11:30 p.m. due to the northern latitude.

Even the smallest events loom large in memory and bring a warm feeling. For instance, I can remember one year bringing the TZ750 sidecar outfit before one of the Isle's notoriously demanding tech inspectors. This fellow noticed some small irregularity on our machine. I claimed no knowledge of the violation, but this touched off the tech inspector like a match head. "You see that boat?" he yelled in his northern accent, pointing to the ferry as it left for Liverpool. "I can put you on that boat!" He was more than happy to use his authority if things were not corrected to his liking. To this day it's a phrase I use with friends and racing mates who are IOM followers. "See that boat? I'll put you on that boat!" I've been back to the Island several times as a spectator, and the allure is still there for me. I love the TT as a phenomenon, an epic event, and a part of racing history—even without a large trophy to show for it.

intersection. This invites cars to try to slip in quickly behind the vehicle in front of you, with dire results. By staying back slightly, in plain sight, you can help avoid this hazard. Show your headlight to them if possible.

CARS PULLING OUT FROM SIDE STREETS, ALLEYS, & DRIVEWAYS

In this situation you are traveling down an arterial and a car pulls in front of you from the right—or directly into you. It's the classic T-bone.

In my experience people will wait until you are very close, and then pull in front of you. In their minds they're thinking, "It's only a motorcycle—I can do this." They have no concept of closing speeds and the likelihood of a collision.

How do you guard against such situations? First, when you are traveling at 25–35 mph in town and notice numerous arterials, driveways, and alleys adjacent to your route, a warning light

should go on in your brain. You need to be in a low gear, covering the front brake, and ready for any contingency. If you see a car, look for movements of the front wheel or a person within. Try to establish eye contact with the driver if possible. If the person looks oblivious, switch on your high beam momentarily.

If there are numerous cars parked in driveways along your route, look for wisps of exhaust that indicate the car might pull out. In all these situations, slower speed is your best ally.

GETTING HIT FROM BEHIND

While sitting still in traffic waiting for a light to change, you may think you're safe—but you're not. I like to think I have a built-in 360-degree sight capability. I'm not just looking ahead—I'm aware of threats that might come from any direction. That's the envelope I put myself in.

For instance, if you're coming to a red light, move over slightly. Don't sit right on the bumper of the car in front—leave at least a bike length. These measures supply an escape route should a car threaten to hit you from behind. (When the light turns, I've even had people accelerate in reverse!)

Also, leave it in gear unless it's a long light and you're safely ensconced between cars. Be ready to react to anything they might throw at you! While waiting for a light to change, there might not be a soul behind you for half a mile, but this doesn't mean you're safe.

As a preventive measure pulsate your brake light to ensure that you're seen. Don't assume that the person coming up behind sees you. Be aware that motorcycles use engine braking a lot. This supplies a great means of control, but doesn't illuminate your brake light. You may wish to tap the brakes occasionally and illuminate the light if someone is following closely.

Pedestrian walkways hold similar dangers. You should of course stop for pedestrians, but simultaneously, check behind for rapidly closing traffic. Don't assume that they know you're coming to a stop. In many cases a motorcycle can stop more quickly than a car.

As a side note, watch where you put your foot down at stops. There is often a smear of oil at lights in the number one slot, and you'll spill if

A LEFT-TURNING MOTORIST IS ONE OF THE MOST DANGEROUS SITUATIONS IN MOTORCYCLING.

When approaching a busy intersection, slow a little, downshift, and cover the front brake. Look for signs such as head movements, front wheels starting to turn, or the hood starting to lift as the car begins to cross your path.

NEVER TREAT A FOUR-WAY INTERSECTION LIKE A DRAG RACE START.

Just because you've got the green doesn't mean it's safe. Hesitate that extra moment to be sure of where the other person is going.

this gets on the soul of your boot. Embarrassing and potentially painful!

PARKED CARS

A perfectly serene-looking residential street can hold a menagerie of dangers. For instance, those parked cars to your right should be viewed with caution. If you see a head in one of them, your internal warning system should click on. If the person looks back over his or her shoulder, step it up to high alert and be prepared for a quick stop.

A wheel turning is another sign of impending danger. Also, try to maintain a car-door distance between yourself and the parked cars to your right in case someone opens a door suddenly.

Everything depends on what you see in a fraction of a second. If you ride around in a daydream, you're going to get hurt.

MULTI-LANE TRAFFIC

Contrary to what you might think, statistics show that riding on multiple-lane highways is safer than urban traffic situations. Nonetheless, there are many things to be aware of out there on the highway.

LANE POSITION AND AVOIDING BLIND SPOTS

Your lane position is vitally important. This includes right/left positioning, and your fore/aft location relative to the traffic beside you. The goal is to be seen. Put yourself in the heads of the drivers around you, and ask yourself: Am I visible to them?

With this in mind, don't run the same speed and position as anyone to your right or left—even if it's a comfortable speed. Get ahead of them or even hang back a bit. Increasingly, motorists seem to regard turn signals as a sign of weakness. They just don't bother to use them. Always assume that the person alongside will swerve suddenly, into your lane, with no warning.

Right/left positioning is also important. Ride just to one side of the center of the lane. If you're in the slow lane, ride just right of center; if you're in the fast lane, ride just left of center. This provides the greatest possible space buffer between you and erratic drivers.

DON'T LET THEM DO IT TO YOU! *Try to maintain a car-door distance between yourself and parked cars in case someone opens a door suddenly.*

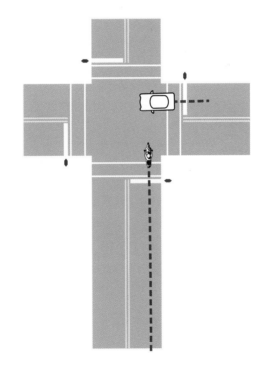

IN MY EXPERIENCE PEOPLE WILL WAIT UNTIL YOU ARE VERY CLOSE, AND THEN PULL IN FRONT OF YOU. *They have no concept of closing speeds and the likelihood of a collision. When you are traveling at 25-35 mph in town and notice numerous arterials, driveways, and alleys adjacent to your route, a warning light should go on in your brain.*

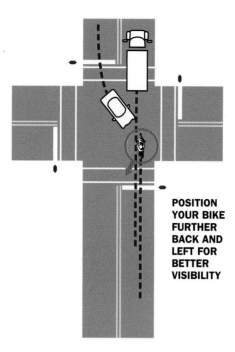

POSITION YOUR BIKE FURTHER BACK AND LEFT FOR BETTER VISIBILITY

LANE POSITION CAN ALSO HELP MAKE YOU MORE VISIBLE TO LEFT TURNERS. *Don't hide behind large vehicles or SUVs as you proceed through the intersection. This invites cars to try to slip in quickly behind the vehicle in front of you, with dire results. By staying back slightly (see the blue arrow in the diagram), in plain sight, you can help avoid this hazard. Show your headlight to them if possible.*

STOPPED AT THE LIGHT. *This rider has put himself in a visible position relative to oncoming, left-turning traffic. He is also visible to the driver in front through the left hand mirror. Always assume drivers may not see you, and use your head to put yourself in the most visible position possible.*

LOOK AT NOTHING, SEE EVERYTHING

One of the most important things in multi-lane traffic is to expand your area of awareness. Is a driver three lanes away doing the dodge-and-dart routine, advancing through traffic? He may be far away now, but he won't be for long. In a fraction of a second, he could be the neighbor you never wanted. Can you see brake lights coming on a mile and a half up the highway? Don't dismiss it. In no time, you'll be staring at bumpers.

Target fixation is a common topic in motorcycle instructional programs. As the theory goes, if you look at something—like a pothole or the road edge—you are more likely to hit it. I've seen this time and again—a rider focuses on a small obstacle, and hits it. Cultivate the skill of looking through the situation, not exactly at it. You need 360-degree alertness.

Ultimately, your safety depends on your detective skills and level of awareness. Is a passenger in the car reading a map? Is someone juggling a cup of coffee and a mobile phone? Are two people in a nearby car engaged in heavy conversation? These are all signs of unpredictability and danger.

Awareness is a skill like any other, and it needs to be developed. With time, you'll begin to take pride in your predictive powers. It can become a game for you. You'll be riding along, and you'll notice a car to your right that looks like it's been in a demolition derby, with the bumper hanging off. You notice the person inside taking a pull from a beer. An instant later, he swerves left, directly in your path.

The good thing is, you're one jump ahead—you've already processed all the information and it spelled *danger*. You've begun to slow down, and when the driver swerves, you're already in low gear. You apply the brakes smoothly, not erratically. What looked like a problem is no problem at all.

FOLLOWING DISTANCE

It's true that today's bikes have fantastic brakes, with awesome power and feel. Compared to the drum brakes of not so long ago, these binders are remarkable. But don't let this lull you into complacency. A lot of riders think, "Well, I have such good brakes, I can outstop cars in an emergency."

Don't count on it. You need to leave ample room between you and the car in front.

Keep in mind that required braking distance increases exponentially with speed. The faster you go, the more braking distance you need. The old rule of thumb works pretty well here: You need at least one bike length per each 10 mph.

It's also critical that you look up and not fixate on what's in front of you. If brake lights come on four cars ahead, start to slow. I call this "ghost riding"—everything in front of me is a ghost. I see it, but I also look right through it. It helps to be in a lower gear, so you can roll off the throttle and get some braking action when traffic is speeding and slowing like this. Remember: rpms are your friend—on the track and in traffic.

MERGING SITUATIONS

Beware around exit and entrance ramps. You can see these huge convergences a half mile ahead, and they should spell "arrangement time" to you. I approach these areas with caution, even when in a car or driving the CLASS Freightliner truck. In these situations, don't trundle along in the slow lane where most of the activity is. If possible, be to the far left. In merging traffic, be prepared for a domino effect, in which the car entering from the far right causes the car to its left to move over, and so on. This situation can spill into your lane very quickly.

Beware of situations in which you and a car two lanes over are switching lanes simultaneously, toward each other. Your 360-degree envelope of awareness should alert you to this situation. Avoid running the same pace and position—preferably speed up and put the hazard behind you.

AGGRESSIVE DRIVERS

Road rage is real, and it gets worse every day. Most of us have witnessed or been involved in situations with irrational drivers.

I won't claim to be an angel. Like everyone else, I have buttons that get pushed every once in a while, and I get agitated. But I try to stay under control.

In the old days, an altercation like this might have resulted in both parties pulling over and having a punch up. These days, people won't just

hit you—they'll *shoot* you. I always remind myself of just how many people carry guns today.

So before you engage that red-faced driver in a roadside argument over motorcyclist's rights, consider the consequences. You may be entirely in the right, but it's not worth your life to make a point. Breathe deeply, curse quietly, and get over it. By the same token, motorcyclists need to take some responsibility to be predictable and not upset drivers with their own poor etiquette. Remember the value of discipline and staying humble in your daily riding.

CARS THAT WANT TO RACE

A related issue involves mountain roads, when motorists observe that there's a motorcyclist behind them. This person is going maddeningly slow in the twisties, where you want to have fun—but they won't pull over on the straights. In fact, they speed up, fully aware of your presence.

Eventually, they may start cutting corners and try to "show you how it's done." Often, this will be someone in a lumbering SUV, and they will be crossing the double yellow, with the tires absolutely screaming, as they try to keep up the pace.

What are your options in these situations? If there's no one behind you, you might just pull

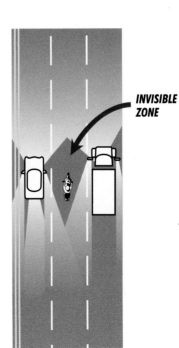

INVISIBLE ZONE

DON'T RUN THE SAME SPEED AND POSITION AS ANYONE TO YOUR RIGHT OR LEFT. *Get ahead of them or even hang back a bit. Always predict that the person alongside will swerve suddenly, into your lane, with no warning.*

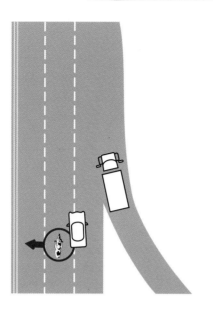

IN MERGING SITUATIONS, DON'T TRUNDLE ALONG IN THE SLOW LANE WHERE MOST OF THE ACTIVITY IS. *Be prepared for a domino effect in which the car entering from the far right causes the car to its left to move over, and so on. This situation can spill into your lane very quickly.*

DO YOU HAVE A PLAN FOR THIS SITUATION? *The pickup pulled out of the driveway and didn't even see this rider coming. But he's got his front brake covered, his rpms are up, and he's in a lower gear—ready for anything.*

over and let the person get up the road. Then you can enjoy yourself once you're underway again.

A related solution has to do with pacing. If you're like me, you find the twisty bits far more fun and engaging than the straights. After all, anyone can pin the throttle in a straight line. Besides making you a magnet for the local constabulary, this WFO (Wide-open, Flat Out) riding only means that you'll catch the traffic in front that much faster—and end up staring at a bumper through the curvy parts. What's the point? A better approach is to observe a sane pace in the straights, and have the twisties to yourself.

TWO HOT TOPICS

Before closing out this chapter, I want to touch on two perennial flash points among motorcyclists and their automotive brethren: crossing the double yellow, and lane splitting.

CROSSING THE DOUBLE YELLOW

Should you or shouldn't you? It's a question every sport rider asks him or herself sooner or later.

It's not hard to understand what's behind the urge to pass someone over the centerline. Imagine it's a beautiful day. You're on your favorite ribbon of tarmac. The road is clear—except for the one slow, very careful driver in front of you. You're thinking: *"I could pass. It would only take a second. Then it would be just me and the open road."*

Get acquainted with the condition of restraint. Good racers know it well. Keep in mind that in general, that double yellow is there for a good reason: limited visibility. I'm no goody two shoes, but let me tell you: *For me to pass over the double yellow, it has to be a 100 percent sure thing.* That's my rule. I don't do it often, but when I do, there has to be no doubt whatsoever of making a clean pass. This means that these conditions are in place:

◆ You have brute horsepower.

◆ You know the road.

◆ Visibility is excellent.

◆ There are no side roads or arterials in the passing zone where someone might pull out or an opposing car might want to turn left.

◆ There are no cars in the opposing lane.

If traffic is moving at more than 55 mph, I suggest restraint. Ask yourself: Do I really need to pass? Don't make passing over the double yellow a regular feature of your riding, or sooner or later it will bite you. And of course, if you get caught, tough luck. There's not much chance you'll be able to smooth talk your way out of it.

LANE SPLITTING

Nobody likes stop-and-go traffic, especially on a hot day. By splitting lanes, a motorcycle can cut through this like a scalpel, getting you to your destination in a hurry. Some riders even feel that lane splitting is safer than riding in the midst of stop-and-go traffic, where you risk being rear-ended.

But lane splitting—going between lines of cars—is not without risks. First of all, it's illegal in most states (California being the notable exception, where it's technically called "lane sharing"). Also, at any moment, a car can swerve into your path, or you can clip a mirror on an SUV or truck.

Since I live in California, I get to choose whether to lane split or not. On the 405 in southern California, coming back from the Los Angeles airport to my home in Santa Paula, it can take 45 minutes to go five miles. You can bet that lane splitting looks very attractive in these circumstances. And I've done it—with great caution, and gobs of control. Here are my cautions:

Only lane split if traffic is moving at less than 20 mph (preferably, less than 10). It's just too risky to split lanes at speed (though that doesn't stop people from doing it, even at 75 mph!).

Use a low gear (first or second). In a low gear you're ready for anything. When you roll off the throttle, you'll slow quickly.

Pick your points carefully. Don't pass a big truck with multiple axles, because in the time it takes to get past the truck, you might get squeezed from either direction and be left with no escape route. A wide car is also a hazard. Also, don't lane split in an area of merges or

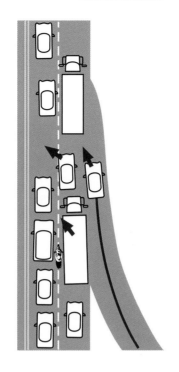

exit ramps. Look for a stable, predictable circumstance, such as passing between two small cars that are adjacent to one another (rather than offset).

Don't make people angry. Don't drop in front of them, slamming on the brakes. As always, try to be a considerate rider. Many motorists already regard lane splitting as rude. Don't fuel the fire with obnoxious behavior.

Get accustomed to riding on raised traffic dots (called Botts Dots). If you aren't comfortable piloting your bike down the road with the wheels going *brrrrr* over the top of Botts dots, then don't lane split.

Be ready for anything. Some people truly hate lane-splitting motorcycles, and will go so far as to open a door on you, spit, or throw garbage out the window. These are the risks you have to face if you want to split lanes. (Don't spit back, especially while wearing a full-face helmet.)

SPECIAL CONDITIONS

DEALING WITH HAZARDS

There are few "ideal" conditions for motorcycling. You have to accept what you're given and make the best of it. There are hazards everywhere. We all hate discomfort, but if you can conquer your emotions, you'll begin to look forward to adverse conditions. (Gold and Goose Photography)

When you encounter that wet, rutted, pot-holed road with a succession of blind corners and the occasional logging truck in the opposing lane, you should find yourself saying: *I can do this.* You'll put your focus and concentration where it needs to be, and you'll enlist the skills you've practiced.

For example, I've done a lot of races in the rain. Many riders would get apprehensive about such conditions, but I always said to myself: *This is great.* Somehow, I turned it into a pleasurable thing. It was a place I could excel. I feel the same way about night riding. Some of my most enjoyable rides have been at night. I love the attitude adjustment and the smells of the evening—along with the challenges.

With the right attitude and skills, you can learn to enjoy—and survive—whatever conditions are thrown at you.

THE JOY OF RAIN RIDING

People are usually surprised to learn that CLASS takes place rain or shine. I tell students that they don't have to ride in the rain, and no one is going to make fun of them if they sit out. But I also tell them that rain presents a wonderful training opportunity. It's the ultimate test of smoothness. Some people don't even shift gears or use the brakes, and that's fine. To get a sense of riding in the wet, they just put it in first or second, and gently roll the throttle on and roll it off. One of our instructors leads them around for a few laps this way—just rolling it on and rolling it off. And you know what? All of a sudden, the scary condition starts to decrease, and their confidence level elevates.

You can attain confidence in the wet, too. With practice, you'll realize that rain riding can be fun—and a great learning experience. You just have to find the right means of control.

When I was growing up in England, I liked to think that my friends and I were just like pilots in the war; we went out in anything, because we had to. Motorcycles were our only transportation, and we weren't going to be late for work or miss a day just because it was raining. We learned a lot of skills that way—through necessity.

You can decide that you won't ride in the rain on public roads, but eventually, you'll get caught in it. Wouldn't it be better to be prepared?

WATCH YOUR SPEED AND KEEP FOCUSED

Racers can turn remarkably fast laps with highly specialized rain tires—often within a few seconds of their times in the dry. But for the rest of us, caution is the watchword. Because traction is decreased and stopping distance is increased in the wet, you need to slow down, particularly in traffic.

A lowside in the rain can happen in a split second. This means you need to be extra vigilant—stay focused and constantly monitor your inputs. A moment's inattention can have immediate consequences in slippery conditions.

EASE UP!

In Chapter 5 I talked about reducing pressure on the handlebar by using weight shifts and pressure on the footpegs and tank (body steering). In the rain, it's even more critical to monitor the amount of pressure you exert on the bar, because traction is decreased. If the handlebar is your primary means of steering, it will get you in trouble. Handlebar input tends to be too abrupt, and will cause the front end to break free in slippery conditions. You need to eliminate tension in your shoulders and arms to avoid giving the front end a bad message.

Time and again, people try this body steering method in the rain, then come back to me and say: "I see what you mean about releasing pressure." By easing up, they find the control they are looking for.

BRAKING IN THE WET

Low gears and throttle management should be your first means of control in the wet. However, with time you can learn to use the front brake very effectively. Gently squeeze it and release it as smoothly as you applied it. Try to get your braking done in an upright position, where traction is at maximum.

EASE UP! *In the rain, it's even more critical to monitor pressure on the bar. If the bar is your primary means of steering, it will get you in trouble. Eliminate tension in your shoulders and arms to avoid giving the front end a bad message. By easing up, you'll find the control you're looking for.*

I don't recommend that riders use the rear brake in the wet. The one exception is if you have ABS—then you can get away with it.

Racers generally have the ability to use the front brake at speed, in the wet, while leaned over. I tell this to students and they say it's not something they want to experiment with. Others have inquiring minds. I tell them they could fall down—some get close to it—but that the experience will build confidence.

This is how racers learn: They make mistakes, crash, and do it again. They're always brushing up against their limits. Of course, I'm not saying you have to crash to improve. But if you want to save your neck, you have to invest the energy. A lot of people are not willing to have that exposure. If you're willing to explore, you'll get better and better. Especially in the wet.

Eventually you'll arrive at a place that's really pleasurable—when you encounter a wet road (or other challenging conditions) you won't be afraid. You'll meet it head on and make use of the tools you've developed.

EVENTUALLY YOU'LL ARRIVE AT A PLACE THAT'S REALLY PLEASURABLE.
When you encounter a wet road you'll meet it head on
and make use of the tools you've developed. (Ian Donald Photography)

OTHER CONSIDERATIONS IN THE WET

Adjust your speed for limited visibility. Rain reduces your view of the road ahead, sometimes dramatically. If your sight distance has closed up, you need to reduce speed accordingly. Imagine that there is a hazard just beyond your envelope of visibility. Should that hazard materialize, you need to be traveling at a speed that will allow you to stop in time.

Watch out during the first few minutes of a storm. This is common wisdom among motorcyclists. Oil and debris make the first moments of rain treacherous. It's better to ride in a downpour that gives the surface a good scrubbing. Don't get too daring too soon. This is also true in racing—nothing is worse than passing someone early in a rainy race, then crashing and being left behind in the mud. It's better to run a little slower and assess the situation.

Tires and tire pressure. Today's tires have changed the whole picture for rain riding. The composition and tread pattern of modern tires provide excellent grip and shed more water than the tires of old. At CLASS, we require students to have virtually new tires, and this is doubly important in the rain. I also find that a slight reduction in pressure puts more rubber on the road and provides more traction. I use 30/30 psi front/rear for a single rider in the wet, compared to 32/32 for a single rider in the dry. (Tires and tire pressures are covered in depth in Chapter 9.)

Dress right. This seems obvious, but what you may not know is that the most harmful effect of being cold and wet is that you lose concentration. If you're thinking about the water seeping into your crotch, or your soaked socks, or your clammy hands, your attention isn't where it should be. There are plenty of good, breathable, waterproof fabrics used to make motorcycle suits, gloves, and boots. Get to know them, and invest a little.

SNOW AND ICE

In England I rode to work all winter. Then I'd go out again in the evenings, to the coffee houses. My friends and I would talk motorcycles and ride some more. We'd be out there on our

NOWADAYS WE HAVE THE TREMENDOUS ADVANTAGE OF ELECTRIC GRIPS, VESTS, AND OTHER EQUIPMENT. *These devices make riding in 30-degree temperatures a joy, and may even open a whole new world of riding for you.*

THE COMPOSITION AND TREAD PATTERN OF MODERN TIRES PROVIDE EXCELLENT GRIP AND SHED MORE WATER THAN THE TIRES OF OLD. *At CLASS, we require students to have virtually new tires, and this is doubly important in the rain. I also find that a slight reduction in pressure puts more rubber on the road and provides more traction (30/30 psi front/rear). (Photo courtesy Yamaha Motor Co., Ltd.)*

Triumphs, BSA Gold Stars, Vincents, and Nortons. Sometimes we'd just toodle along at slow speeds due to the icy, rutted conditions. But we rode no matter what. We actually had fun trying to balance out the bad conditions. It was an era of much enthusiasm!

Should you ride when the weather turns foul? Sometimes you have to. If you get caught in a winter storm and the nearest shelter is miles away, you may have to tough it out. It may be better to ride than to suffer by the roadside and risk hypothermia.

The technique in these conditions is much the same as for rain: emphasize lower gears and throttle management. Avoid sudden inputs through the handlebar—use body steering. Search out the pavement sections with the most traction, such as automobile wheel tracks, and avoid extreme lean angles.

And, as in all adverse conditions, you need to harness your emotions and release the tension. At times, conditions will be so bad that common sense will tell you to get off the road. It's important to listen to this voice in your head. One of

these situations is freezing rain. In these conditions traction is near zero, and a motorcycle simply cannot turn without being able to apply a side force on the tires. You need to draw the line on that one. When the temperature is close to freezing and the roads are turning to ice, pull in.

COLD

It's important to monitor yourself in cold weather. If you become very cold, your reaction time will suffer, and that can spell danger in traffic. Cold hands and feet may impair your shifting and braking. Stop frequently if you need to, and don't plan to go as far as you would in better weather. Use good judgment.

Nowadays we have the tremendous advantage of electric grips, vests, and other equipment. (You can add these to almost any bike—most modern alternators can easily handle the additional electrical load.) These devices make riding in 30 degree temperatures a joy, and may even open a whole new world of riding for you. Here in California, some roads are less congested, the scenery is great, and the crisp air is wonderful to breathe in winter. It's a great time to ride.

HEAT

The key to riding in extreme heat (90 degrees or more) is to maintain concentration. Our minds tend to wander when we're uncomfortable—just like in the cold stuff. If you can't focus, then it's time to get off the road, have a cool drink, and recover. Be aware of the signs of heat exhaustion, including cramps, nausea, or light-headedness. If you experience these symptoms, it's time to park it for a spell.

For long rides in the heat, many riders have success with backpack-style hydration systems, which put a drinking hose close at hand and enable you to hydrate while riding. In the absence of this, pull over periodically (every hour at least) to drink. Open whatever ventilation flaps you have, and perhaps try wetting yourself down under your protective gear. Lane splitting is a tremendous temptation in the heat, because it causes at least a little breeze to pass over you. (Remember, lane splitting may not be legal in your state.)

CROSSING TRACKS. *If the railroad tracks are going nearly the same direction as you are and traffic does not permit you to approach at a different angle, the key is to relax on the bars and get across quickly.*

SHOULD YOU RIDE WHEN THE WEATHER TURNS FOUL? *Sometimes you have to. If you get caught in a winter storm and the nearest shelter is miles away, you may have to tough it out. It may be better to ride than to suffer by the roadside and risk hypothermia. (Photo Courtesy John Hermann)*

HOW I BECAME A RAIN MAN

ENGLISH WEATHER WAS MY TEACHER

Years spent riding in and around London confers special abilities on a rider. For instance, to this day, I can smell rain before it happens. The scent fills my nostrils and the next thing you know, drops begin to strike the pavement. A useless skill? Maybe, but it's an uncanny ability shared by many Brit motorcyclists—a sixth sense for precipitation.

Rain is woven into all my motorcycling memories from that time. Rain in summer, rain in the fall, rain in winter. Rain turning to ice, my Triumph Thunderbird skittering around underneath me, my feet splayed like outriggers to keep from falling. Rain with my girlfriend riding pillion, on the way to the ACE Cafe, cursing me for my miscalculation (didn't smell it that time).

We didn't have high-tech fabrics, or electrics, or any of the other comforts taken for granted today. My sole defense against the elements was a big, three-quarter-length Belstaff wax-cotton jacket—the Gore-Tex of the day. A strap extended down in back, which I would pull up under my crotch, helping to exclude the worst of the weather. Since rain could blow in off the North Sea at any moment, I kept the prized Belstaff bungeed to my tank. This was the standard "kit" for this rider, along with waterproof overboots and gloves. For riders of the day, it worked.

Practicality didn't always win out. Many stock British bikes came with enormous, valanced mudguards that were extremely effective in keeping the worst of the muck off of bike and rider. Naturally, we stripped them off in favor of smaller, more fashionable polished alloy race types (or "ali," as we called it). In the mind of a teenager in the '50s, coolness won out every time.

We rode in the rain because we had no choice. When bikes are your only form of transportation, as they were for me, you just do it. When it's time to go to work, and the rain is coming down in buckets, you wheel it out. In England, it's just another day. Time to ride.

After a while, a curious thing begins to happen. You begin telling yourself you actually like it. Providing you were dressed for the occasion, it wasn't half bad. And after a while, you realize you're getting good at it. The more you relax and release the tension, the easier it becomes. This is true of most things in motorcycling, but especially rain riding.

There is no doubt that being schooled in English weather paid dividends later in my career. Rain became a strong suit for me. In 1978, at the American Federation of Motorcyclists' Six Hours of Ontario, it rained for about 4-1/2 of the six hours. I was riding the big, 140 horsepower Vetter Kawasaki KZ1000. Our team led the race early, before the worst of the rain came. Since we were on slicks and other teams were on street tires, we actually lost the lead for the middle part of the race. But before long, the rain started to lighten up, and I managed to unlap the field. Coming into the

Years spent riding in and around London confers special abilities on a rider. The rain is woven into all of my motorcycling memories. Rain in the summer, rain in the fall, rain in the winter—my Triumph Thunderbird skittering around underneath me. You have to love it, mate! (Photo courtesy Bob Branam)

final lap, I took the lead again, and actually won the big event by just a few seconds. It was amazing to come onto the home straight after all that time, see the leaders in front of me, and overtake them.

For that win, and many like it, I credit a lifetime of riding in the rain, and skills derived from the best possible teacher—necessity. I credit riding across rain-soaked cobblestones, tram lines, and manhole covers. I credit England.

RACES TO REMEMBER

ONTARIO 1974

Nothing comes free in racing—every lap is a fight for inches, and an unrelenting search for some tiny shred of advantage. Can you lay off the brakes a fraction of a second longer than you did the previous lap? Can you stuff your wheel up the inside of the guy in front of you, or will he slam the door and leave you with nowhere to go? Can you let the back end drift a little longer on the next corner exit, and suppress the gnawing fear of a highside?

These are the things a racer thinks about every lap, every moment. The guy who wins is usually the one who conquers his own better judgment and allows himself to stretch the envelope to the max.

But very rarely—maybe only a few times in a racer's life—everything just falls into place. These are

the moments a racer lives for. I was presented with such a gift at the AMA Heavyweight Production road race at Ontario, California, in 1974. The mood was great along with excellent weather and a friendly team atmosphere.

For this race I am riding the Butler & Smith BMW R90S twin, prepared by Helmut Kern. Famed tuner Udo Gietl also flies out the day before, specifically to help Helmut prep the big beemer. The two tuners work through the night to get the machine in shape and to my liking.

Race day gets closer, and on Friday I go through a routine I know so well: a few practice laps to scrub in some spare tires, switch wheels, then a few more laps to warm up the actual race tires. When I pull in, Udo comes over expectantly and

asks what else I might need. He is accustomed to finicky racers, but today, I am not one of them. The bike is *perfect,* I tell him.

The BMW is running such high compression that oil sometimes blows past the piston rings and fouls the plugs, and so it's become my habit to always have a new set installed before a race. I ask Udo to do this for me—but nothing more. In every other regard, the bike could not be better. Udo is a bit incredulous at how easy I have made things for him, but he does as I ask and screws in the new set of plugs.

Yvon Duhamel on his Yoshimura-built Kawasaki Z1 is the race favorite, having won every production race thus far in the season. Steve McLaughlin is another strong challenger, joined by Wes Cooley,

It all came right. Ontario in 1974 was one of those races where everything just clicked. The bike was flawless—a good combination of suspension and tires—and I felt confident and made it show. A great win! (Photo courtesy Reg Pridmore)

David Emde, and Mike Baldwin. But today, I have something they don't have. Right from the start, I open up a lead. I put my head down and don't look back. Each time I come past the pits, the board says just one thing: *plus.* I just keep going. Again: *plus.* I'm liking that word more and more.

By the time the flag drops, I have a 20-second margin. I take a cool-down lap, come back in, and proceed to the winner's circle after taking position on the number one spot. Just then, Duhamel pulls in. He looks at me in a puzzled way, then says, "What are you doing here?"

"What do you mean, what am I doing here?" I tell him. "I won the race!" He didn't even know that I had pulled my disappearing act and left both he and McLaughlin in the dust.

It was one of those days where everything just clicked. The bike was flawless—a good combination of suspension and tires—and I felt confident and made it show. (Although afterward I had to proceed to the ambulance to take 10–15 minutes of pure oxygen, because the Ontario smog used to hurt me bad.)

It was a great victory for me—one to remember. The one that came easy.

Jason at five years old was my biggest fan! After winning big at Ontario he enjoyed being in the winner's circle with Dad. (Photo courtesy Reg Pridmore)

One thing I don't allow myself to do in heat is shed my protective gear. I remember one summer ride in Atlanta that was well over 100 degrees. Some people there choose to ride unprotected. It's a personal choice, granted, but not a good one. I just lifted my shield, loosened my collar, and tolerated it. People in cars looked at me like I was crazy, but I did it.

WIND

Wind can be very fatiguing. I gauge the wind by letting it move me. This gives me a better idea of its strength. Sometimes I feel as if I'm bobbing around like a cork on the ocean. But it's important to remember not to fight the wind through the handlebar. This kind of tension causes fatigue, overreaction, and abrupt movements. This can cause the front end to break traction.

When winds approach 40–50 mph—especially if it's a gusting crosswind—you may need to park it. In these instances, the wind can literally move you halfway across the road. It's too dangerous.

Another situation to avoid is when you emerge from a tunnel, ravine, or other obstruction that serves as a wind block. Be ready for the sudden gust that can follow. A passing big rig can produce the same effect.

YOUR FIRST LINE OF DEFENSE AGAINST DEER AND OTHER WILD ANIIMALS IS TO PLAN AHEAD. *Granted, some encounters are totally unavoidable, but I believe that the majority of such collisions occur because riders are asleep at the switch.*

NIGHT RIDING

I've always loved night riding—particularly by moonlight. I used to do it a lot in England. You should experience what night riding has to offer. The sights and smells are fantastic. Where I live, near Ojai, California, the smell of oranges and lemons is strongest at night. I've also been across the California desert at night when it's cold and clear, and been treated to a spectacular display of stars, especially in Death Valley.

One obvious caution is to reduce speed enough so you can perform a quick stop within your sight distance—in other words, don't "overdrive" your lights. Equipment is also important. Higher-powered halogen bulbs and auxiliary lights are available for many motorcycle models, and can increase your sight distance dramatically. You need to stay warm, using adequate insulation, warm gloves, and electric clothing if you have them. Another trick is to tilt your head down slightly when confronted with bright oncoming lights—this can diffuse the glare.

OTHER HAZARDS

There are so many hazards you need to be aware of in your daily travels: everything from slick paint stripes, to manhole covers, to potholes, to abrupt road edges.

Each one requires a little different technique, but there is one principle that will serve you well no matter what you encounter: the ability to release tension. If you can master panic, it will transform your ability to deal with these hazards. You need to let the bike do what it has to do, rather than fight it through the handlebar. Gradual inputs—using your full body instead of your arms—are far less likely to disrupt handling or cause the bike to break traction. If you can learn to relax in this way, chances are you'll come through cleanly. Some specific hazards include:

METAL PLATES

These are used to cover holes in construction areas, and can be very dangerous when wet. If you must cross one, imagine that your hands are almost off the bar. The natural tendency is to tense up and grip the bar harder, but this can produce abrupt steering and cause the front end to wash out.

RAILROAD TRACKS

Cross these at a right angle if possible. If the tracks are going nearly the same direction as you are and traffic does not permit you to approach at a different angle, the key is to get across quickly. If you slow, your wheel will have more time to abruptly deflect, which may cause you to go down.

ROAD DEBRIS

As a rule I don't follow behind open pickup trucks or any vehicles carrying a high, stacked, or loose load. You never know what's going to fly off. If you must follow such a vehicle, even for a short time, don't tailgate. Leave plenty of distance. Another bad one is the "gator"—huge tire pieces thrown off by 18-wheelers. These can get kicked up by a car and land right in front of you. The best prevention is to extend your awareness and your following distance. If you see cars swerving around something, even a half mile up the road, it's time to move into high alert.

PEDESTRIANS AND CYCLISTS

Many pedestrians feel that the world is going to take care of them. They'll walk right into the street and act like they're invincible. With this in mind, be aware that a casual walker on the sidewalk may suddenly step into your path. Give them the right of way, but don't put yourself in danger, either. The car behind you may not see the pedestrian, and when you stop suddenly, you'll be rear-ended. Use your 360 degree awareness.

Bicycle riders are another potential hazard. I practice good etiquette and afford them a lot of room. Be aware that not all cyclists stick to a straight line—one second they will be on the road edge, and the next they'll be in the middle of the lane. That's why you need to plan and leave adequate spacing.

ANIMALS

Your first line of defense against deer and other wild animals is to plan ahead. Granted, some encounters are totally unavoidable, and I've heard some horrible stories of collisions with wildlife.

DOGS ARE A CONSTANT THREAT TO MOTORCYCLISTS. *If you see a dog you can usually slow enough to assess the situation, then use your bike's horsepower to leave the dog behind.*

But I believe that the majority of such collisions occur because riders were asleep at the switch. They weren't doing what they were supposed to: riding with a plan and focusing on the situation at hand.

You need to read the signs: If you're passing through a forest, particularly during a full moon, extend your awareness to the road edge. Look for subtle movements or the glow of a pair of eyes. Cover the front brake. Reduce your speed and use a lower gear. Also, this may be one time when you want to follow a car rather than pass. Let another vehicle light your way to safety and assume the collision risk for you.

With smaller animals and reptiles—squirrels, snakes, and the like—I don't take strong evasive action. I hate to hit them—*g-dunk, g-dunk*—but sometimes I will if I have to. It's not worth the risk to run into oncoming traffic or off the road.

Dogs are a constant threat to motorcyclists. I've even hit one—a glancing blow—and managed to stay upright. If you see a dog you can usually slow enough to assess the situation, and then use your bike's horsepower to leave the dog behind. Whatever your strategy, it's critical that you don't fixate on the dog and veer into traffic as a result.

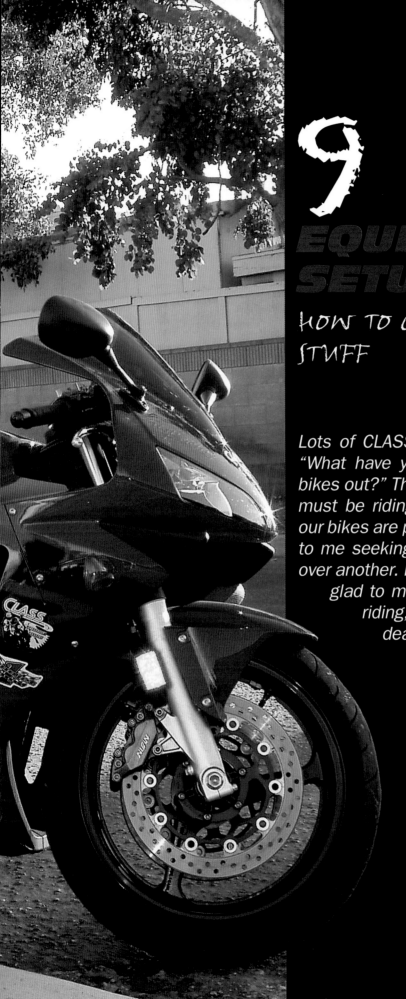

9

EQUIPMENT, SETUP, & GEAR

HOW TO CHOOSE THE RIGHT STUFF

Lots of CLASS students approach me and say, "What have you done to trick your instructors' bikes out?" They figure since we're going fast, we must be riding something special. The truth is, our bikes are pretty stock. Riders frequently come to me seeking advice on the merits of one bike over another. I don't have all the answers, but I'm glad to make use of my almost 50 years of riding, racing, and being a motorcycle dealer to furnish a few pointers.

Motorcycles are incredibly competent these days. They accelerate, stop, and handle better than ever before. And they're extremely reliable. The truth is, it's hard to choose a bad machine from one of the major makers.

Don't base your choice on bragging rights. Buy the size and type of bike that suits your style. At CLASS we take all kinds: sportbikes, cruisers, tourers, streetfighters—you name it. We do require a displacement of 250cc or larger, to ensure that the bikes can go uphill at a reasonable speed.

If there is one recommendation I make frequently, it's to start small. I often meet riders who say they haven't ridden since owning a 125cc dirt bike 20 years ago, but nonetheless they decided to buy a 1000cc sportbike. Then, predictably, they fall off twice in one week. What possesses people to make such a big jump? It's just asking for trouble.

Those who are re-entering the sport or who feel at all nervous about motorcycling should start small. There are some very good 250s, 500s, and 650s out there. Riders with short inseams may also want to opt for smaller bikes. I don't recommend that short riders decrease the fork or shock lengths, because such changes adversely affect handling and may cause hard parts to touch down in corners.

Also, keep in mind that it's not mandatory that you be able to touch the ground while seated. Many riders adapt by studying the camber before rolling to a stop and putting a foot down on the high side. It's also helpful to slide your bum off the saddle slightly to make the reach.

Spouses also need to resist the urge to buy a large bike just because a husband or wife has one. I see this often at CLASS: The husband has a 1000cc, and dammit, the wife is going to have one, too. Bad idea. The same thing applies between you

A DETAILED MECHANICAL INSPECTION PRECEDES EVERY CLASS. *I always ask participants if they have checked their tire pressures. Fully half of them either don't know or tell me it's 40 or 50 psi because "that's how the dealer inflated them." You should educate yourself and exercise control over the mechanical aspects of your bike, just as you exercise control over your riding! (Ian Donald Photography)*

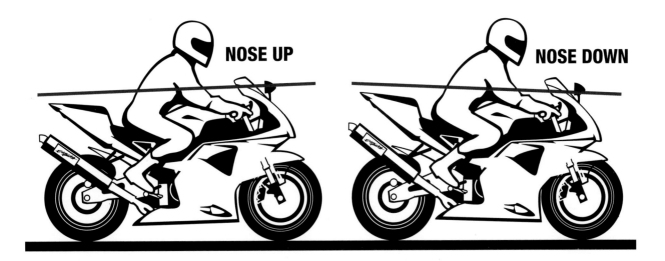

NOSE UP   NOSE DOWN

and your riding friends. Don't get a bike for bragging rights—get the one that suits you.

MAINTENANCE

Get in the habit of performing a simple inspection of such basic things as tire pressure and fluid leak. At the start of every CLASS session, I ask participants if they've checked their tire pressures. Fully half of them either don't know or tell me it's 40 or 50 psi because "that's how the dealer inflated them." Over-inflation can supply a harsh ride and reduce traction. (I recommend 32 psi for most conditions.) Everyone should look at their tires at least once a week, checking for wear or embedded objects.

I've always been a cleaning nut. While I'm at it I notice screws that are missing, fluid leaks, and the like. I don't want sloppiness in my riding, and I don't want nuts and bolts falling off my bike. Aerobatic flyers are very strict when it comes to preflight routines—their lives depend on it. They have a wonderful way of going through a whole 5–10 minute inspection before they go up. It's just one more way of exercising control. Motorcyclists should do the same.

Out on the street, small mechanical problems can be disastrous. We've had people come to CLASS tech inspection with their chains as tight as can be. They tell us that's how the dealer set it. It will come as a rude surprise when the chain snaps and goes through the crankcase or hits them in the leg!

My point is not to criticize dealers—after all, I was one for 23 years. But you need to educate yourself and exercise control over the mechanical aspect of your bike—just as you must exercise control over your riding. You shouldn't be at the mercy of someone else—whether it's a mechanic, or the driver in front of you.

SUSPENSION

I'm amazed at how well stock suspension works on most of today's bikes. Before you rush out and buy expensive aftermarket shocks, experiment with what you have. It may be that you need special components such as a stronger spring or something with greater damping adjustability. But don't make the mistake of putting on a huge spring just because someone told you to, or for bragging rights. Your bike may end up riding like a rock.

When we acquire new bikes for CLASS, I try to see what I can get out of the stock setup by tinkering with compression and rebound damping, and by adding a little preload for cornering clearance. The result is usually quite good.

However, consider changing a rear shock if it's used in competition. When you use a shock that aggressively, the damping may fade and never get a chance to give you its full potential. Aftermarket shocks use cooling reservoirs and other technology to help maintain their temperature and damping characteristics during hard riding.

SUSPENSION SETTINGS AFFECT SAG. *Sag is the amount the suspension compresses at rest. This, in turn, affects the bike's attitude: whether it's nose down or nose up. Attitude affects weight bias: whether you have more weight on the front or back wheel.*

REG'S MECHANICAL CHECKLIST

TOP. *Check your chain weekly. Vertical play should be one-half to three-fourths of an inch. Too tight or too loose are both bad and could result in catastrophic failure. Lube regularly and wipe off the excess.*

BOTTOM. *With your bike on the center stand, you can check several things (in addition to the chain). Spin the tire and check for wear or embedded objects. Put a hand on the top and bottom of the wheel to check for bearing play, and move the wheel laterally to check for wear in the swingarm pivots. Spin the wheel to ensure that the bearings roll smoothly.*

When it comes to wrenching, some folks have natural interest and skill—while others could care less. Through the years, I've noticed three levels of mechanical aptitude (or the lack of it!):

THE FETTLER: These guys would rather spend time cleaning and wrenching than riding. Some airplane pilots are like this, and I've seen a lot of them come through CLASS. These guys leave no stone unturned. With their planes, they do a walkaround before every flight, checking the undercarriage, making sure the elevator and rudder move, running a hand over the fuselage. With their motorcycles, they take the same approach. Their bikes are spotless, the oil is fresh—even the tires are clean. (Truth be told, I'm a fettler—and a pilot—myself.)

THE COMMUTER: These guys take good care of their bikes—but only enough to ensure that they can continue logging 1,000 miles a week. They change the oil regularly,

but might be guilty of a slack chain once in a while. They might also try to squeeze a couple extra hundred miles out of a tire. But their bikes are basically sound.

THE SLACKER: These are the guys you want to avoid. Their bikes have bone-dry batteries, which means the normal starting protocol is to park facing downhill and give it a good shove. The tire pressure is down in the teens, and the rear brake light has been out for a month. The chain flops around deliriously, preparing to commit hara-kiri into the crankcase. The tire could be mistaken for a racing slick—except for its square profile.

I'm not recommending that you be like any of these riders, because all of them are excessive in their own ways. I'm only asking that you do the right thing for your enjoyment and safety—and that of your passenger. You need to educate yourself and exercise control over the mechanical aspect of your bike, just as you must exercise control over your riding.

HERE'S MY PERSONAL LIST OF THINGS TO CHECK REGULARLY:

WHEELS AND TIRES
You should inspect your tires at least once a week, checking for wear and embedded objects. You never know when you might pick up a nail on the street. Track riders aren't immune either—I've often seen a flat caused by an embedded piece of safety wire picked up in the pits.

Perform this check by putting the bike up on the centerstand (if you have one), and running your hand over the tire while turning it slowly. Ensure that the wear bars are still visible and that you have adequate tread, especially for wet weather riding.

Check tire pressure often, preferably once per week. I recommend 32 psi front and rear for most conditions with bikes weighing 400–600 pounds. For heavyweight bikes, use 36 in back and 34 in front. Also, pay attention to a drop in pressure. If your tires are dropping 4–5 pounds per week, you may have something embedded in the casing.

With older bikes, it's a good idea to put a hand on the top and bottom of the wheel and push and pull to check for bearing play. (Modern bikes with sealed bearings don't seem to suffer this problem quite so much.) When your wheels are off, take a moment to spin the axle and check for bearing smoothness. If your bike has spoked wheels, run a screwdriver lightly across them as you turn the wheel, checking for a musical pitch. If you find an off note, you may have a loose spoke. You can also check this by squeezing each pair of spokes with your fingers.

CHAIN

Check this weekly, especially if you are a commuter and do many miles per week. Total vertical travel should be 1/2 to 3/4 of an inch at the tightest point. I prefer to apply WD-40 penetrating lubricant over the length of the chain, and wipe off the excess. Be sure not to overdo it with lubricants of any variety.

FRAME

Ensure that the handlebar turns freely from left to right with the front wheel elevated. If there are stops or hesitation, you may have pitted head bearings. This can severely affect handling.

Check the operation of the side-stand and centerstand, ensuring

OIL. *These days we're lucky to have plainly visible oil sight windows, which means there is no reason to ever let your oil drop below the recommended level. I never bring my oil up to the top indicator line. It's better to keep it slightly below.*

that the springs are in place and the stands snap back to their resting positions. With most modern bikes, the engine will not run with the sidestand down when you engage first gear. Be sure this feature is operational by kicking the sidestand down periodically with the engine running and first gear engaged. If not, check the operational switch. Some stands also have grease nipples, which you should inject with lubrication periodically.

OIL

These days we're lucky to have plainly visible oil sight windows, which means there is no reason to ever let your oil drop below the recommended level. Overfilling is almost as bad, because it can harm engine internals. In fact, I never bring my oil up to the top indicator line. It's

better to keep it slightly below. Also, look for leaks and puddles on the floor each time before you ride.

GAS

Check your gas before every ride, or have a plan for your next fill-up. Obvious? Yes, but you'd be amazed at how many problems this causes on group rides and especially at the track, where aggressive riding at high rpms can drain a tank in short order. It's no fun to push a bike home on the street, and it's no fun to have a track day cut short by an empty tank. Check your tank and plan ahead.

THROTTLE

Ensure that the throttle is free and that it snaps closed on request, and that the cables aren't binding (indicated by a rise in rpms when the handlebar is turned).

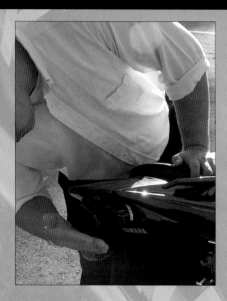

LIGHTS ARE LIFESAVERS, PLAIN AND SIMPLE. *Periodically check your taillights—both the running lights and the brake light. Be more visible and avoid a ticket: replace burned out bulbs.*

LIGHTS

Lights are lifesavers, plain and simple. All new motorcycles today are required to have always-on headlights, and for good reason—it's been statistically shown to decrease one of the worst types of accidents: the dreaded left-turning motorist. Check all of your lights frequently, operate the turn signals, and ensure that the brake lights come on with both brakes.

BRAKE PADS

Check your pads periodically or at the same time you check your tires—at least once per week if you ride regularly. City riders in particular tend to go through pads quickly. Use a flashlight if necessary, ensuring that the wear grooves are still visible front and rear. Brake shoes in older bikes with drums could use an inspection from time to time.

BATTERY

Riding regularly is one of the best things you can do for your battery. If you don't use your bike weekly, invest in one of today's excellent automatic chargers and use it often (these chargers make it impossible to overcharge). Ensure that the electrolyte is between the marks and covering the cell plates. (Most modern batteries are sealed so electrolyte does not have to be checked.)

In my experience, if your battery is older than three years, you're riding on borrowed time. Cold weather can shorten this interval. If you notice slow starting with a battery that's older than three years, consider investing in a new one. Even better, have it tested at a shop.

COOLANT

Modern, well-maintained bikes rarely use much coolant. Still, it's worth checking to see if the level is between the marks indicated on the overflow tank (don't overfill). Do this while the engine is cold. While you're at it, check the condition of hoses and fittings.

NUTS, BOLTS, & ADJUSTERS

Once per month, or when you're performing other service, take a few minutes to put a wrench to such things as triple crown and axle pinch bolts, chain adjusters, exhaust mounting bolts, bar-end weight mounting bolts, fender stay bolts, and the like. It can be pretty dramatic to have a muffler or some other part come off and get tangled up with moving parts (i.e., wheels).

CABLES

Older bikes have a lot of cables to tend to (brakes, clutch, throttle). Check the condition at the attachment points, and look for kinks that might cause binding. Periodically use one of the small cable lubricators to run some oil down inside the housing.

Modern bikes have far fewer cables (due to hydraulics), and the cables they do have are generally lined with nylon or some other means of permanent lubrication, and so don't require much attention.

LUGGAGE & RACKS

If you're traveling with a load, check to ensure that rack mounting bolts are tight, and that the gear is securely held in place. Having an old, worn-out bungee break and go into your rear wheel would be disastrous. Worse yet, losing all of your personals on a busy freeway will definitely ruin a trip!

THE IMPORTANCE OF GETTING YOUR HANDS DIRTY

I have to admit something here, I'm a bit of a cleaning nut. In my past days I made sure to present a clean, professional racing image. It's much the same today. I keep my everyday equipment in presentable style—like somebody cares! But it's not just about image. By getting my hands dirty, I can reassure myself of the best chance of finding something amiss and correcting the problem before it makes trouble.

This attitude won a lot of races for me, but it also helps me enjoy this great sport of ours on a daily basis. Hopefully a little dirt under the fingernails can do the same for you, too

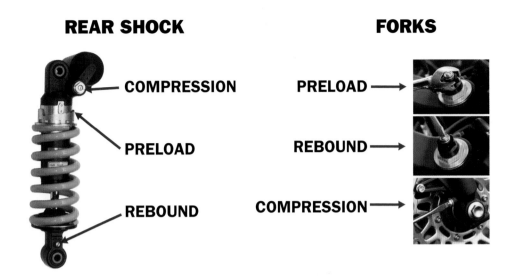

REAR SHOCK

COMPRESSION

PRELOAD

REBOUND

FORKS

PRELOAD →

REBOUND →

COMPRESSION →

SUSPENSION PRIMER. *Preload is the compressive force applied to the spring at rest, governing the point at which the spring begins to work. Damping supplies resistance to the action of the spring. Compression damping governs the spring's movement under load; rebound damping affects the speed at which the spring returns to its original position.*

ENVISION WHAT THE BIKE IS DOING

It's important to envision what's happening with your suspension and the effect that any changes will have. The objects are to keep the wheels on the ground, and the chassis stable. Sometime, watch a semi-truck going down the road. When the suspension is working correctly, the load is stable (little vertical movement) but the wheels are moving up and down and the shocks are working hard. Because a motorcycle and its load are so much lighter, the settings must be made more sensitively, but the dynamics are the same.

We see riders at CLASS whose rear wheels are getting airborne over rough sections, or who are practically being ejected out of the saddle by excessive spring action—obvious signs of a setup problem.

A SUSPENSION PRIMER

There are two main means of adjustment. Preload is the compressive force applied to the spring at rest, usually via a threaded adjuster that bears down on the spring. It governs the point at which the spring begins to work—a higher preload will require more force to initiate movement.

Damping supplies resistance to the action of the spring, preventing it from behaving like a pogo stick. There are two types of damping: compression, which governs the spring's movement under load, and rebound, which affects the speed at which the spring returns to its original position. Damping occurs by passing oil through small orifices in the fork or shock. Damping is

increased when the orifices are reduced in size or closed off entirely.

A bike with a spring that's too stiff or that has too much preload will get slightly airborne over bumps. Too much compression damping can have the same effect. Too much rebound damping will prevent the wheel from returning to its original position after hitting a bump.

Suspension settings also affect sag, which is the amount the suspension compresses at rest. This, in turn, affects the bike's attitude—in other words, whether it's nose down or nose up. Attitude affects weight bias: whether you have more weight on the front or back wheel.

That's a lot to consider, and you can make yourself crazy with minute changes. Racers have computer feedback to tell them exactly what's happening at every point of the track, in every condition. There is no end to the changes they make.

Fortunately for the rest of us, setup just requires common sense. I have a simple procedure that has served me well through many years of riding and racing. Usually, when I introduce CLASS students to this procedure and make a few changes to their bikes, they come back and tell me they can't believe how much better the ride is. Here's how it works:

STEP 1: ADJUST PRELOAD/SAG

A lot of riders have an impulse to make the ride stiffer with a stronger spring and more preload. But too much preload or spring won't allow compliance over bumps, and the wheels won't

LIFT BIKE
FROM REAR

HAVE FRIEND
HOLD BIKE
FROM FRONT

MEASURE FROM
HARD POINT TO
HARD POINT

ADJUST REAR PRELOAD.
Grab a frame rail toward the rear of the bike and see how much you can lift it. Then let it fall to its resting position. Do this several times to assess the amount of sag. To adjust rear preload, use the special wrench in your toolkit to turn the preload ring against the spring (or use a hammer and punch). Retest it with each adjustment. I recommend half an inch of "sag" in back at most—even less if you ride two-up with a heavy rider in back.

stay in contact with the ground. You need to tailor the settings to your bike and riding style.

Rear Preload. Push your bike off its centerstand or sidestand and position yourself alongside while holding the left handlebar. With your right hand, grab a frame rail toward the rear of the bike, and see how much you can lift it. Then let it fall to its resting position.

Do this several times to assess the amount of sag. You should have half an inch at most—even less if you ride two-up with a heavy rider in back. If you have an inch or more, that's wasted travel—you've already lost a significant amount before going down the road. And since the bike sits lower with too much sag, you'll lose cornering clearance.

To adjust this, use the special wrench in your toolkit to turn the preload ring against the spring (or use a hammer and punch). Retest it with each adjustment.

Front Preload. Stand alongside the bike and pull in the brake lever. Push up and down on the handlebar a couple of times then lift up on the bar, and allow the front end to settle and find its natural position. Then, with the front brake still on, pull up and back, and let it settle again.

As with the rear, there shouldn't be more than 1/2 to 3/4 of an inch of movement. To modify this, turn the screw-type adjuster atop the fork legs. Use small increments, and retest with each adjustment. (Not all bikes have adjustable fork preload.)

Preload and sag affect another important aspect of handling: the attitude of the bike. Imagine a line drawn through the axles, parallel to the ground. The rear of the chassis should be elevated relative to this line—in other words, the bike should be slightly nose down.

A bike with too little rear preload (excessive sag) tends to make the front end look like that of a chopper. Within limits, attitude can be adjusted via preload. Most often, you need to decrease preload slightly in front and increase it slightly in the rear to achieve the right chassis attitude.

Some "upside-down forks" can be slid upward in the crowns in order to lower the front end. (Upside-down forks have lower sliders that travel inside the upper fork stanchions, instead of the reverse. You can easily tell if this is the case on your bike because the lower part of the forks will be of a narrower diameter than the uppers.) This is a very effective way to lower the front end, but it can be overdone. Don't drop the front down too low, or you'll place too much weight on the front tire.

STEP 2: ADJUST DAMPING
When it comes to damping, it's important to realize what's happening inside the suspension. A lot of people think suspension is just a spring. If this were true, the bike would bounce uncontrollably,

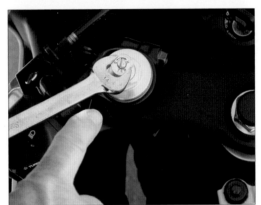

ADJUST FRONT PRELOAD. Stand alongside the bike and apply the front brake. Push up and down on the handlebar a couple of times then lift up on the bar and allow the front end to settle and find its natural position. Then, with the front brake still on, pull up and back, and let it settle again. To adjust front preload, turn the screw-type adjuster atop the fork legs. Use small increments, and retest with each adjustment. (Not all bikes have adjustable fork preload.) As with the rear, there shouldn't be more than 1/2 to 3/4 of an inch of movement.

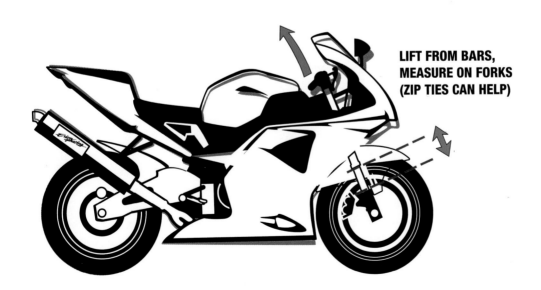

LIFT FROM BARS, MEASURE ON FORKS (ZIP TIES CAN HELP)

FRONT DAMPING AD-JUSTMENTS ARE MORE ACCESSIBLE THAN EVER. *It only takes one fourth of a turn to make a noticeable change in compression damping (top) or rebound damping (bottom). Be sure to note your starting positions and record any changes, so that you can revert to the original settings if necessary. If sharp bumps are transmitted directly to the handlebar, you may have too much compression damping. If your bike seems to lose suspension action over a washboard surface, you may have dialed in too much rebound damping—in other words, the spring is being compressed more and more over each bump, but it is not being allowed to spring back quickly enough to its original length.*

like a pogo stick. Damping is what governs the speed of the spring's action—both in compression and rebound. It keeps the suspension under control.

A sure sign of insufficient damping is a bike that feels like a pogo stick—it goes *boing, boing, boing* down the road. Other cues are subtler, and you need to envision how the suspension is working over the bumps to understand how you can correct any problems.

If your preload is set correctly but sharp bumps are still transmitted directly to your butt or the handlebar, you may have too much compression damping. On the other hand, if you get rocketed out of the seat after every bump, your bike may lack rebound damping (the spring is snapping back too fast). If your bike seems to lose suspension action over a washboard surface, you may have dialed in too much rebound damping—in other words, the spring is being compressed more and

more over each bump, but is not being allowed to spring back quickly enough to its original length.

The types of damping adjusters and the amount of adjustability vary greatly from one bike to another. Some forks have no damping adjustability. (This is not to say they have no damping—just no adjustability.) Others have rebound adjustments only, or a single adjuster that governs both. The best forks have both types of damping adjustments—the rebound adjuster is usually atop the fork legs, and the compression adjuster is at the bottom of the fork legs.

Rear shocks may have adjusters for rebound and compression, or a single adjuster that governs both. Usually, these latter systems have a greater effect on rebound than compression. For instance, the adjuster may have a 60 percent effect on rebound, and a 40 percent effect on compression. Consult your owner's manual for the details.

Damping adjustments have a profound effect, so don't just rush in and make radical changes. Three "clicks" of a screw type adjuster can make the bike unmanageable. Keep a record of every change and its effect, so you can return to what you had originally if it doesn't work out.

BRAKES

When it comes to brakes, the old adage "out of sight, out of mind" applies for most people. As long as the brakes function, riders don't give them much thought. Brakes are a regular part of our morning tech inspections at CLASS, and they should be part of your pre-ride regimen, too. You need to take action before your pads make metal to metal contact.

Most brake pads are extremely easy to check (with the exception of those on some full-dress tourers). Simply take a flashlight, shine it at the pads where they meet the disk, and ensure that the wear grooves still have some depth. Also, always check your pads when you have your tires changed and the pads are out and in plain sight.

Should you use stock or aftermarket pads? If you don't feel you're getting enough performance from your brakes, I recommend sintered (metallic) pads, which give significantly better performance and won't harm your disks.

Over time brake fluid absorbs moisture, which impedes performance. Periodically inspect the fluid in your reservoir and ensure that it's a clear or gold color (not brown). Regardless of what your fluid looks like, you should flush the system and replace the fluid once per year.

CHAINS

I remember a time when maintenance involved removing the chain, soaking it in hot paraffin, and then reinstalling it with a new master link. Thankfully, those days are gone. Today's O-ring chains are extremely sophisticated and durable. O-ring chains have lubricant that is permanently sealed within the roller. If one of these chains doesn't last, it's usually due to poor maintenance.

Start by examining the chain for tight spots as you turn the wheel with the bike up on the centerstand or workstand. If there is a severe tight spot, you need to replace the chain, or it will pull on and damage the final drive or rear wheel bearings. A severely tight chain will break, with sometimes catastrophic results, such as locking up the rear wheel or putting a hole in the crankcase. Total vertical travel should be 1/2 to 3/4 of an inch.

I recommend that you put rags under the chain area, apply WD-40 penetrating lubricant over the length of the chain, and wipe off the excess. Keep in mind that the lubricant doing the real work is already sealed inside the chain. The goals of regular maintenance are to keep the chain clean and ensure that the O-rings don't dry out. For these purposes, I find WD-40 works very well.

EXHAUST SYSTEMS

I have mixed emotions about aftermarket exhaust systems. I love a good crisp exhaust note on a multi-cylinder bike. I also think that a slightly louder exhaust can help make your presence known in traffic—though many people argue otherwise. In addition, aftermarket titanium or carbon exhausts look great, and can offer considerable weight savings.

However, I appreciate the fact that noise pollution is a problem for motorcycling in general. Many riders go to an extreme and buy the most obnoxious pipes available, and I frown on that. It damages our already strained relations with the non-riding public. Especially avoid loud pipes if you live in a densely populated neighborhood or trailer park. One of the tracks we visit with CLASS—Laguna Seca—has strict noise regulations. Many riders have been told to quiet it down or leave for exceeding the 92-decibel limit.

I've also found that many aftermarket systems offer only small performance advantages

MOST BRAKE PADS ARE EXTREMELY EASY TO CHECK. *Simply take a flashlight, shine it at the pads where they meet the disk, and ensure that the wear grooves still have some depth.*

LEFT. *Always check your pads when you have your tires changed and the pads are out and in plain sight.*

RIGHT. *Over time brake fluid absorbs moisture, which impedes performance. Periodically inspect the fluid in your reservoir and ensure that it's a gold color (not brown). Regardless of what your fluid looks like, you should flush the system and replace the fluid once per year.*

THE BMW R90S

HOW WE TURNED AN "OLD MAN'S BIKE" INTO A SUPERBIKE CHAMPION

How much performance can you get from a bike? You'd be amazed. My 1976 BMW R90S—considered by most people to be an "old man's bike"—showed the way. Although the R90S was BMW's attempt to enter the sportbike realm, it was still basically a tourer, better suited to carrying luggage and a passenger than winning an AMA Superbike championship. But what could we do? What do race teams ever do in these situations? You take what you are given and you set to work. My Butler & Smith team, and our fantastic tuner Udo Gietl, performed miracles in 1976.

Step one was to breathe some fire into the motor. The stock two-valve-per-cylinder, air-cooled horizontal twin could only rev to 7,200 rpm and produce about 67 horsepower. To reach the desired 9,000 rpm, the valvetrain would need major upgrading. This included hollow, titanium pushrods, hollow valve lifters, and an aftermarket camshaft. To raise the horsepower, the cylinders were bored 1mm over standard (giving close to 1000cc total displacement). This required big, aftermarket pistons, which were mated to titanium connecting rods and custom-made wrist pins. After extensive work on a flowbench, the inlet and exhaust tracks were reworked. We used larger diameter inlet and exhaust valves, plus auto-style racing valve springs with titanium retainers. The airbox was removed in favor of velocity stacks hanging off the massive 40mm Dell'Orto carburetors. A twin-plug ignition was created to fuel the fire. A custom oil cooler was added to help the raging motor keep its composure in the heat of battle, and to resist cavitation (pumping air instead of oil). To take advantage of the narrower powerband, a customized, close-ratio gearbox was fabricated (five speeds for some tracks, four speeds for others). The finishing touch was to create a dry clutch to save weight. Voila! A fast, powerful (almost 100 horsepower), but fragile motor capable of winning superbike championships—as long as it didn't blow up!

Of course, that was just the motor. The chassis, while known for its good manners on the street, was far from race-ready: the drive shaft (no chain) tended to jack up the rear end under acceleration and the huge, protruding jugs frequently touched down in corners—a fact that was readily apparent from ground-away portions of the valve covers. To address these woes, the motor was moved in the frame to provide more clearance and improve weight distribution. We shortened the cylinders to provide more ground clearance (and to increase compression). Adjustable Koni shocks were added in the back. Large, wide rims were spoked up to accept larger tires, with an offset to clear the driveshaft tunnel of the swingarm. Bracing was added to the frame, forks, and swingarm, to improve stiffness. Forks were revalved. To add yet more cornering clearance, I changed my riding style dramatically by using the hang-out-to-dry method (hanging off).

A thousand minor miracles were performed by Geitl and his team, all with an eye toward winning a Superbike championship. Was their magic enough to turn lead into gold? My '76 AMA Superbike title, the first ever awarded, says that all the hard work was worth it.

My 1976 BMW R90S, prepared just like teammate Steve McLaughlin's (shown here), was considered to be an "old man's bike," but was fast enough to produce my '76 AMA Superbike title! (Photo courtesy the AMA)

over stock. Today's stock pipes are extremely efficient. In general, a full aftermarket system offers more potential for a performance advantage than a slip-on.

TIRES

Radial tire technology has changed the way we ride. Today's tires stick incredibly well and enable us to use fantastic lean angles. However, we want conflicting things from our tires. We want them soft for adhesion and cornering, but we also want them to last longer.

Some racers can trash a set of tires in 100 miles, while others have a riding style that allows them to get 5,000–10,000 miles. The constant heating and cooling cycles of any tire can cause the inner construction of the tire to deteriorate, causing the contact with the road to become questionable and dangerous. Pay attention to the condition and pressure of your tires. They are your lifelines.

Fresh tires are important to your safety, especially in the rain. At CLASS we require students to have new tires, and this means 95 percent of tread remaining. We occasionally turn people away for having poor tires. We take this issue very seriously—after all, your life depends on those two small contact patches.

I'll state my blatant prejudice here: I've used Dunlops for many years and prefer them. For one thing, they match my riding style, because I like adequate strength in the sidewalls to prevent "squirm" in corners. I also find they don't need to be heated up as much as other brands do, which is good for CLASS since we are frequently on and off the track and ride in all types of weather. Dunlop is always on the development edge. I have a lot of faith in Dunlops, plus a lot of race wins to my credit using its products.

What about tire pressure? Though many sportbike tires indicate 40 psi on the sidewall, I recommend 32 psi front and rear on road and track when cold. If you are two-up with a heavier rider in back (180 pounds or more), use a pound or two more in the rear.

I also have a rule of thumb: Take the pressure when the tires are cold, then take it again when it's hot. It shouldn't rise more than 10 percent. If it does, your tires are underinflated. If it only

I LOVE A GOOD CRISP EXHAUST NOTE ON A MULTI-CYLINDER BIKE. *I also think that a slightly louder exhaust can help make your presence known in traffic. At the same time, I appreciate the fact that noise pollution is a problem for motorcycling in general. Be smart about it. (Photo courtesy Erion Racing)*

TODAY'S TIRES STICK INCREDIBLY WELL. *They enable us to use fantastic lean angles. I recommend 32 psi front and rear on road and track when cold. If you are two-up with a heavier rider in back (180 pounds or more), use a pound or two more in the rear. (Photo courtesy Dunlop Tire Corporation)*

IF I'D ARRIVED AT THE ACE CAFÉ LOOKING LIKE THIS IT WOULD HAVE ENDED IN A PUNCH-UP (FIGHT)! *The truth is, today's helmets are life-savers. I suggest buying a name-brand, full-coverage helmet that meets the Department of Transportation (DOT) or Snell Memorial standards. Those simple requirements will ensure a good level of performance in a crash. (Top photo courtesy Reg Pridmore. Bottom, left photo courtesy SHOEI Safety Helmet Corporation. Bottom, right photo courtesy Buell Motorcycle Company)*

rises one or two pounds, your tires may be over-inflated. For instance, if a tire at 32 psi cold measures 36 or 37 when warm, you may wish to experiment with a slightly higher pressure. If it only indicates 33 psi when warm, you may wish to reduce pressure.

The important thing is to make tire inspection and maintenance a regular part of your regimen.

In CLASS we frequently ask people when they last checked their tires—some can't even remember doing it. That's bad. Check pressure weekly, and take the time to look for slits or embedded objects. You'll be glad you did.

RIDING GEAR

In CLASS I always emphasize the importance of good riding gear. I've fallen off several times at 100-plus mph, and those incidents have taught me the value of having the best.

Of course, I realize most people have financial constraints, and a complete outfit can be expensive. For instance, at the upper end you will pay $2,000 for leathers, $800 for boots, $600 for a helmet, and $300 for gloves. But think of it this way: Your total investment would still be less than the cost of a couple of nights in the hospital, which is where you might end up if you use poor equipment.

Someone is always willing to make gear cheaper, or worse. Don't seek out that 15-year-old jacket just because it's stylish. In a crash, the stitching will come apart faster than an F-14 Tomcat and the next thing you know you'll be nursing serious road rash. You may only need your gear one time—but when that time comes, it will be worth it to have the best.

HELMETS

Helmets are offered in a dizzying array of models, designs, and color schemes. How do you know which to choose? For starters, you should buy a name-brand, full-coverage model that meets the Department of Transportation (DOT) or Snell Memorial standards. Those simple requirements will ensure a good level of performance in a crash. A top-of-the-line helmet, with superior padding, sound protection, and ventilation, will cost $400–$600. I don't recommend an open-face helmet. Nor do I recommend a hinged helmet (the ones where the front opens). I don't believe they have the same strength and integrity as a one-piece model, although they are certainly better than an open-face unit.

Fit is critical. Your helmet should be on the snug side, especially when new. With time, it will conform to your head slightly. A snug helmet is more likely to be there when you need it—a loose one can actually be ripped up and over your head in a crash.

Regardless of their quality, helmets need to be replaced every five years, because the polystyrene material that absorbs the impact degrades over time. In CLASS we display an old helmet that has been cut in half, and you can actually dig your finger into the material and see how it disintegrates. Think of it this way: If you spread your $500 investment out over five years, it will look like a bargain. At CLASS, helmets are part of our normal tech inspection at the start of the day. You should make it part of your daily regimen, too.

I prefer a tinted shield for all types of riding. I even use a mildly tinted shield at night, to reduce glare. In mid-summer I use a dark shield, or one of the new shields that eliminate damaging ultraviolet rays. Some riders who require prescription lenses wear glasses under their shields, but I tend to avoid anything that presents a sharp protrusion in a crash.

How should you put your helmet on? I'm sometimes surprised at how many people don't know the drill. It's simple: Put your left index finger through the D ring, grasp the right strap with your right hand, and spread the straps as you put the helmet on and secure it. Lace the right strap through both D rings, and back through one. Make sure it's reasonably snug—in a bad accident, a loose strap will come past your chin and the helmet will fly off. Don't forget to secure any loose ends so they won't flap and become an annoyance and a distraction.

LEATHERS

With leathers, you really do get what you pay for. I've seen people get hurt with $500 full leathers made out of soft material that offers virtually no resistance to abrasion. The leather wouldn't stop a thing. On the other hand, I've seen riders crash at 100-plus mph in top-of-the-line, $2,000 leathers who have brushed themselves off and said, "Thank you very much!" Throughout my career, I've always used the best that money could buy—and I'm still in there, mate.

The best leathers are made of quality cowhide and use superior, double-stitched seams. The stresses imposed at 100 mph are awesome, and only the best construction will withstand this. All CLASS instructors use Helimot leathers. This is not a blatant plug for a sponsor—we pay for these suits. I've seen the way this company double stitches the seams to

THIS RIDER LOOKS CONFIDENT, AND IT MAY JUST STEM FROM THE GOOD GEAR HE'S USING. *I recommend you purchase the best that money can buy! The finest leathers are made of quality cowhide and use superior, double-stitched seams. The stresses imposed at 100 mph are awesome, and only the best construction will withstand this. (Photo courtesy Helimot Inc.)*

TOP. *Having broken my wrist in crashes, I can tell you that it's no fun. In many instances, good gloves with wrist bracing will prevent this. The best gloves offer more than just protection—they have superior fit and feel that you will appreciate every time you ride. (Photo courtesy Helimot Inc.)*

BOTTOM. *In my racing career I suffered a double compound fracture of the lower leg, and later a broken right ankle. I feel sure that if I had been using one of today's boot designs, I wouldn't have had these injuries. In retrospect I would have paid any amount to avoid all that pain and anguish! Boots need to support the ankle in a way that doesn't allow the foot to be gyrated in or out. I call these "security boots." (Photo courtesy Helimot Inc.)*

provide inner strength. Helimot leathers have protected a lot of riders, and I certainly give them my stamp of approval.

I encourage people to get a custom fit, especially if your shape is different from the norm. In addition, custom leathers are usually of higher quality. If you are buying off-the-shelf leathers, always try them on and ensure that the arm length, leg length, and knee pad position is correct. Ensure that the calves and arms aren't too tight, because these areas tend to pump up when riding. Look for adequate padding and protection at the shoulders, elbows, hips, and knees.

What about synthetics? Suits made of ballistic nylon or Kevlar are perfectly acceptable for CLASS and your daily riding. Many of these suits also have the advantage of being water resistant, and can fit over regular clothes for commuting. However, for me, nothing beats leather for protection and comfort. I have a synthetic oversuit I use for rain riding (on top of leathers), but for impact and abrasion protection I rely on leather.

Spine protectors that fit under your leathers are also a good idea. I prefer types with soft foam padding to those with big, articulated plastic pieces ("armadillo" types), which in themselves can be a source of abrasion or injury in a crash.

GLOVES

Good gloves offer more than just protection—the best ones have superior fit and feel that you will appreciate every time you ride. Expect to pay close to $300 for the very best. Having broken my wrist in crashes, I can tell you that it's no fun. In many instances, good gloves with wrist bracing will prevent this.

Look for quality, durable kangaroo leather with metal studs in the palm, and a gauntlet-style design that extends well beyond the wrist. Gloves should also have some type of padding or protection in the area of the knuckles, such as Kevlar or carbon fiber. There should also be a retaining strap and elastic band at the wrist to ensure a tight entrance. My personal set also has carbon wrist braces. Never buy gloves that are too large. To test this, try to push the opening of the glove down over your wrist with the opposite hand. This should be difficult or impossible. A tight fit and retaining strap will ensure that the gloves will be there when you really need them.

What about cold weather? My preference is to use my normal, high quality gloves with synthetic overgloves to provide an additional layer. I avoid heavy ski-type gloves because of the loss of sensitivity at the controls, and because most models don't offer the same degree of protection as your regular gloves.

BOOTS

In my racing career I suffered a double compound fracture of the lower leg, and later a broken right ankle. I feel sure that if I had been using one of today's boot designs, I wouldn't have had these injuries. In retrospect I would have paid any amount to avoid all that pain and anguish.

Motocrossers have proven through the years that a boot needs to support the ankle in a way that doesn't allow the foot to be gyrated in or out. I call these "security boots." The upper portion of the boot (above the ankle) should pivot but not allow lateral movement. Top-of-the-line boots with this feature and the best quality materials can cost as much as $800. Beware of look-alikes and ask yourself this question: Why do they cost so much less? Look for compromises that could endanger you in a crash.

What about street riding boots? Keep in mind that you can just as easily break your ankle at 30 mph on the street as you can at 110 mph on the track. Still, some makers offer a version of their security boots that feature more freedom of movement for walking. At the very least, your street boots should include the rigid ankle support I described.

JUST LIKE HAVING THE BEST TIRES, GOOD GEAR WILL PAY OFF SOMEDAY IN YOUR RIDING FUTURE. *You can't know when or where it might occur, but when it does, you'll be glad you invested in the best money can buy. Synthetics are OK, but for impact and abrasion protection I rely on leather. I also recommend a spine protector that fits under your leathers. I prefer types with soft foam padding to those with big, articulated plastic pieces ("armadillo" types), which in themselves can be a source of abrasion or injury in a crash. (Photo courtesy American Honda Motor Co., Inc.)*

10

TWO-UP & GROUP RIDING

TIPS FOR SAFELY SHARING YOUR SPORT

I enjoy two-up riding, and I do a lot of it, both on the road and the track. Not only is it pleasurable, but it's also an excellent test of smoothness. It's a great feeling when you and your passenger are working in concert on a strong bike, leaning into corners and enjoying the day. On the other hand, if the two of you are at odds, going down the road clanging helmets, then maybe you need to work on your smoothness! (Kevin Wing photo courtesy Motorcyclist magazine)

THIS COUPLE LOOKS COOL AND READY FOR BUSINESS. *Although his and hers matching blue jeans can result in road rash that won't be forgotten for a long time! (Photo courtesy Yamaha Motor Co., Ltd.)*

For many years CLASS included a mid-day opportunity to ride on the back of my bike, during the lunch break. I've conducted thousands of these "e-ticket" rides through the years. For a lot of people it was an opportunity to go faster than they ever had before—a real eye opener. But I didn't do it to scare them. I did it to help them understand the value of smoothness. Some of these pillion riders actually watched my hands to learn how to better operate the brake, clutch, and throttle simultaneously. They also experienced lean angles they never thought possible, and discovered how much they can trust a pair of tires in a corner. It gave them a new perspective on their own riding and what they might be capable of doing.

Over the years students expressed so much interest in being better two-up riders that I even conducted a special CLASS session to teach these skills—for two-up riders only. It required special permission from the track (Streets of Willow), and I believe it was the first time it had ever been done. We had a great day.

RIDER RESPONSIBILITIES

What makes a good two-up rider? First is a sense of caution and respect for your companion. You need to assess your passenger. For some people, a ride on the back is very exhilarating. They enjoy the speed factor. For others, it can be very scary. It's your job to gauge this before getting under way, by asking your rider about their experiences and preferences.

One of your most important responsibilities is to keep your ego in check. Never try to impress your passenger or condition them to your accustomed speed. Not only is this dangerous, but they may never want to ride with you again (or with anyone else, for that matter).

Being a responsible two-up rider also means accounting for the added weight and its effects on turning and stopping. Since the total package has more mass, you'll need to apply the brakes harder and allow more stopping distance. You'll also need to educate your passenger about the various methods of holding on. If you're carrying an unfamiliar passenger, make sure you get used to their movements and effects on the bike. Fatigue is another issue to be aware of because two-up riding can really wear you out due to the added weight, so moderate distance and saddle time accordingly.

PILLION RESPONSIBILITIES

You should get the bike off the sidestand or centerstand and be comfortably seated with both feet down and the front brake on before allowing anyone to get aboard. Settle in and give the word OK to board. A tall passenger may be able to swing the right leg over the bike and put both feet on the passenger pegs simultaneously. A shorter rider will need to stand on the left peg and swing his or her right leg over, and for this you need to be well braced with the left foot down and the bike straight upright. The passenger should put a hand on your back or shoulder for balance while climbing on. Both of you should give a thumbs up or verbal OK when ready to get underway. On the track or for sport riding, pillion riders should:

Reach around and place the hands on the tank. This way passengers can support themselves under any braking conditions rather than forcing you to support them with your arms. If they cannot comfortably reach around to the tank, they should push on the small of your back during hard braking. Don't have them push on your upper body, which requires that you support them with your arms and affects your use of the controls.

Squeeze with the elbows. Those passengers who are able to place their hands on the tank should squeeze the operator's torso with their elbows under acceleration. This will help keep them planted in the middle of the saddle under hard acceleration. Those riders who can't reach around to the tank should simply grasp the operator's waist under acceleration.

TOP. *There are many great helmet-mounted passenger communication devices available now. Some are simple intercoms; while others interface with bike-to-bike radios, music systems, cell phones, CB radios, and the like. I support using anything that helps keep you awake, aware, and working in unison on the bike. (Photo courtesy Chatterbox)*

BOTTOM. *For fast two-up riding, the passenger can reach around and place his or her hands on the tank. This provides support under any braking conditions rather than forcing you to support him or her with your arms. (Ian Donald Photography)*

THE WORLD OF SIDECARS

In the 1950s I worked for a three-store chain outside London called Reg Smith Motorcycles. (Nice name.) Part of my job was assembling sidecars. But don't get the wrong impression—these were not fully faired, competition-style outfits with gobs of power and fat slicks on the back. These were modest twins or even singles, gasping under the load of big, heavy, fully enclosed sidecars.

In those days sidecars were the U.K. equivalent of the Volkswagen bus in America, enabling a family of four to take an economical holiday. The outfit might have a full canopy to keep the evil English weather at bay, and a spare wheel and luggage lashed to the back. To better enjoy the long trip, the family would make tea along the way and sip happily while bumping down the country lanes. Top speed of these modest units was 65 mph—with an English gale at your back.

No matter. I loved them. Sidecars have always had a special attraction for me, from those early days, through my racing career, and especially including my experiences on the famed Isle of Man. Sidecars demand the utmost from pilot and passenger in smoothness and coordination—and they deliver tremendous satisfaction when it all comes together right.

Part of my job while a teenager was to assemble sidecar outfits, or chairs as we fondly called them, from new. Most British bikes of the day included what looked like a big hole in the midpoint of the frame, where you would attach fittings for the sidecar. The procedure also included changing to stiffer fork springs to support the load, and adjusting the camber to compensate for the narrow, crowned roads. This last adjustment was tantamount to an art form, and involved placing long boards against the wheels to judge alignment, and performing subtle tweaks to the fitments to get it just right. Adjusted properly, an outfit set up this way could be ridden hands off for only a very short period on a flat surface—but go dead straight on the typical British roads. Perfect.

The shop also owned an outfit we called the "float"—a flatbed sidecar used to pick up disabled bikes. Periodically we would receive a call from a despondent rider whose BSA, Triumph, or Norton had ingested a valve or suffered some other debilitating fate. In these instances we would cheerfully hop aboard the float and perform a rescue. A crate was mounted to the sidecar, into which the dead motorcycle would be placed via a folding ramp and then lashed down for its journey to the shop and eventual repair. No tow trucks for us! But it was great fun to practice different cornering techniques with the poor old BSA M21 float.

Those were my pedestrian beginnings in sidecars. Now, fast forward to 1966. My next encounter is borne of necessity, as a means to recover from the horrific crash I suffered earlier the previous year on a solo

Sidecars have always had a special attraction for me. They demand the utmost from pilot and passenger in smoothness and co-ordination—and they deliver tremendous satisfaction when it all comes together right. That's me and Kenny Greene at the Isle of Man. **(Photo courtesy Reg Pridmore)**

Before the 1981 Long Beach Brand Prix, we heated up the crowd with some great sidecar action. Here, Kenny Greene and I lead the way in front of 25 sidecars from around the world. (Photo courtesy Reg Pridmore)

racer. I have very limited range of motion in my badly broken right leg, which is knitted together with steel wire and a Threadall. The outfit provides a nice, easy sitting position from which to convalesce.

In no time, I am hooked. I love the feeling of speed, and the big outfit provides the perfect entree back into the sport. Before I know it, I am racing sidecars and solos, almost every weekend. Once a racer, always a racer, I guess. The need for speed is deep and irrepressible. (Sex wasn't bad but speed was safer.)

My first racing outfit is what we call a "sitter," which provides a relatively upright position as I recover from my injury. The bike is a "Triton"—a Manx Norton frame with a pre-unit Triumph motor (separate gearbox and crankcase).

Before long, I convert this rig into a "kneeler," which provides the traditional lower, more aerodynamic racing position. I also install a more modern unit-construction Triumph 650cc motor, courtesy of John McLaughlin. All of sudden I have a new animal, and am winning club races. The fact that my little Triumph is beating monstrous, 1300cc Harley-Davidson outfits makes it even more satisfying.

Of course, it's not just me winning races. For my first years in the sport I am fortunate to have an enthusiastic passenger named Ernie

Caesar at my side. We ride every weekend, splitting the expenses and winnings evenly, enjoying ourselves immensely. Ernie becomes like a brother to me, and we share the hard prep work along with the fun of winning.

By '67 my solo career is back on track (pun intended), but I love sidecar racing so much that it becomes a whole new focus. But with focus comes intensity, and before long I feel the need to upgrade the rapidly aging Triton. As if to confirm this thought, in one race, the rear wheel collapses as we push the bike harder and harder. Oops.

Enter Rob North, the famed builder of BSA and Triumph factory racers for the likes of Mike Hailwood, Gary Nixon, and Don Emde. Rob has been a sidecar racer and he knows what it takes to develop power and make the big chairs handle. The basis of this new outfit is a Yamaha TZ750 two-stroke, four-cylinder motor. On the back we are running a fat slick, and the power is sufficient to light it up at any corner exits.

The rig is so powerful, in fact, that our biggest mechanical challenge is to keep the final drive from self-destructing under the load. We fabricate a setup consisting of a chain leading to a universal joint adapted from a Honda Civic. We also install a primitive version of a

linked braking system. There are five calipers total: three in front, one on the rear wheel of the bike, and one on the sidecar. Depressing the foot pedal activates the rear sidecar units and one on the front, while pulling the lever activates two front calipers. The braking power is awesome—good thing, too. We need it. At the Isle of Man, with my new passenger Kenny Greene, we are clocked at 142.35 mph down to Creg ny Baa. Thrilling—especially on a road not much wider than your average lunch table.

Through it all, the real attraction to the sport is the teamwork and camaraderie involved. Late at night, in the garage, we do "dry runs." I sit on the bike, making embarrassing motor noises to simulate shift points, while Kenny makes his well-timed moves on the sidecar. The whole thing seems a little goofy (good thing the door is shut!), but it works. And it's essential that I don't cause him to lose a handhold or foothold around the 37-3/4 mile IOM course. Like good athletes, we practice until we get it right. We have to. On the Isle of Man, descending Bray Hill at triple-digit speeds, there is not time for tea or even a warm beer!

149

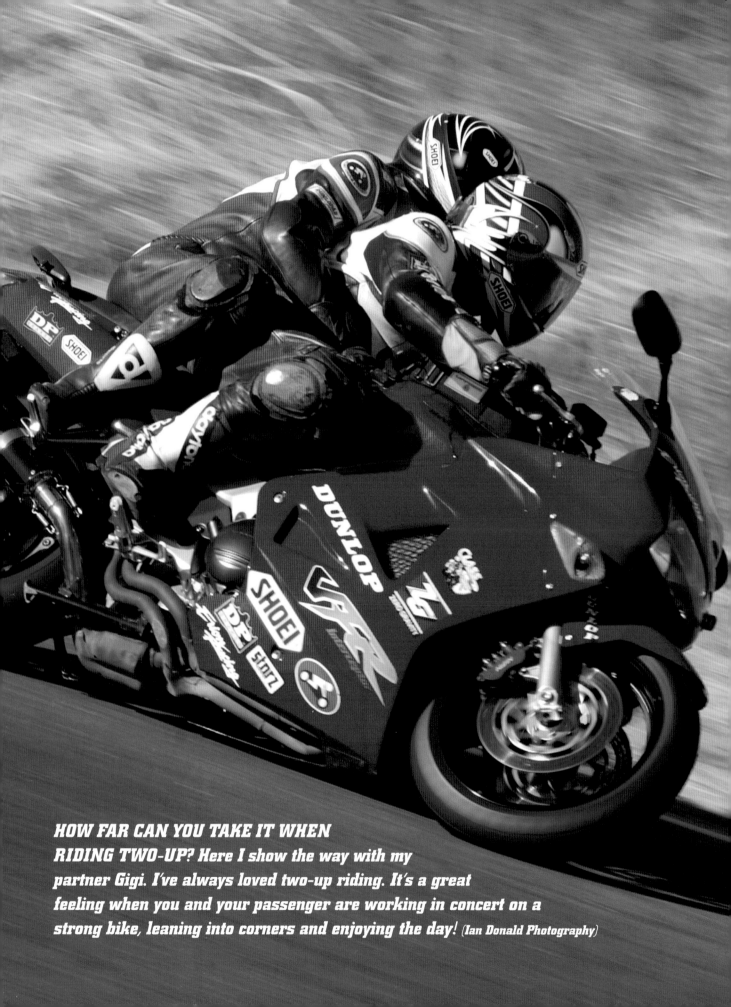

HOW FAR CAN YOU TAKE IT WHEN RIDING TWO-UP? Here I show the way with my partner Gigi. I've always loved two-up riding. It's a great feeling when you and your passenger are working in concert on a strong bike, leaning into corners and enjoying the day! (Ian Donald Photography)

Use proper foot position. Passengers should keep the toes up (not pointed down) and the balls of the feet on the pegs. This ensures that their boots don't touch the ground in corners (for aggressive sportriding), and provides a good foundation for weight shifts and moving around in the saddle. (Riders aboard cruisers or big touring bikes with footboards needn't pay attention to this.)

Look through the corner. Passengers should keep their eyes level with the roadway, turn their heads, and look through the corner—just as the operator does. This is critically important, as it directly influences body position, ensuring that the operator and passenger move in unison. It all starts with the eyes and head! Work together.

Don't be a wet sack. Being a passenger at a sporting pace isn't a passive role. No daydreaming, please. The passenger needs to be an active part of the rider/machine combo, and not daydream.

Many passengers on Honda Gold Wings and other large touring bikes might contest that last point. In fact, some pillion riders see nothing wrong with taking a nap back there in that big old armchair. In my opinion this is a dangerous practice. Snoozing riders on the back will negatively affect handling—especially at a sporting pace. They may also endanger themselves in the event of a quick stop or evasive maneuver. This doesn't mean they can't relax and enjoy the scenery. But at all times, passengers have a responsibility to be an integral part of the package. This also includes traffic and road awareness. Passengers should also take care not to distract the pilot with a constant refrain of "Look at that!" This type of distraction could cause an accident.

There are other niceties that passengers can perform. For instance, when I pull into a gas station, my partner routinely helps pull the bike up on the centerstand, then goes around to the front and unlocks the gas cap. I have no objection to that! And it makes me feel that she's part of the proceedings.

COMMUNICATION

Every couple develops their own sign language on the bike. On the track, I tell people to dictate the pace by giving me a thumbs-up or thumbs-down. I always heed this, since I want it to be a pleasurable experience for them and not exceed their comfort levels.

On the road, a unique language will develop. With my partner, a pinkie in the air means it's time for a cup of tea. A tap on the tank means it's time to refuel. Pointing to an upcoming sign or exit means it's time for a bathroom break. It's particularly important for the passenger to indicate when he or she is going to stand or stretch a leg. Otherwise these movements may surprise the operator.

There are many great helmet-mounted passenger communication devices available now. Some are simple intercoms while others interface with bike-to-bike radios, music systems, cell phones, CB radios, and the like. I support using anything that helps keep you awake, aware, and working in unison on the bike.

EQUIPMENT AND ADJUSTMENTS

Here are some equipment-related tips to keep your two-up riding safe and comfortable:

Choice of motorcycle. It's possible to ride two-up on most sport bikes—but on some, passenger comforts are minimal at best. For instance, a Honda CBR954RR is a fantastic sport bike, but the pillion accommodations may land you in

RIDING TWO-UP. *Passengers should keep their eyes level to the roadway, turn their heads, and look through the corner—just as the operator does. Note how relaxed my arms are—bent, not straight. (Ian Donald Photography)*

divorce court. This is due to two primary factors: minimal seat padding, and high, rearward pegs. Passengers on this bike, and others like it, will be complaining about sore, bent knees after the first hour. If you plan to do extensive two-up riding, shop around and talk to those who have used various bikes for the purpose. It's possible to get a great sporting motorcycle that serves both purposes. A few that come to mind include the Honda VFR 800, the Honda ST 1300, and some BMW models, but there are numerous others.

Tire pressure. Tire pressure should be checked at least once per week. In general, you should add pressure for two-up riding. The amount depends on the weight of the passenger and luggage, but a good rule of thumb is to add two pounds in the rear, making it 34 psi in back, and 32 psi in front. Added pressure will also help keep hard parts from dragging in the corners. Honda Gold Wings and other big tourers weighing as much as 800 pounds need to run at least 36–38 psi in the rear, and 34 in front.

SAFE GROUP RIDING. *The key to safe group riding is exercising your self-knowledge. You need a firm understanding of yourself and your capabilities. If you can't resist the urge to follow a faster rider, you'll end up in trouble. (Ian Donald Photography)*

Suspension settings. It's a good idea to add a little preload in front and even more in the back for two-up riding at a sporting pace—how much also depends on the weight of passenger and luggage. The most important thing is to keep hard parts from scraping. If you touch anything down—even once—address the problem immediately by adding preload. Touching down parts will throw you down the road before you know what hit you. Don't take the chance. If you ride two-up extensively, you may even want to consider a stronger spring in back.

Clothing and protective gear. Just because you're riding two-up and at a more relaxed pace doesn't mean you can forgo good protective gear. Use the same level of protection that you would riding single, and invest in the same gear for your partner. It's also important that the passenger not make adjustments to clothing or gear while riding. Clothing should be secured before leaving whenever possible.

GROUP RIDING

I spent my career racing inches from other riders at triple-digit speeds, so you'd think I'd be comfortable riding in the relative calm of a group ride on the street. Truth is, I've never been much of a group rider. For me to ride in a group, I need to know and have a high degree of trust in the other riders. I don't want anyone to do anything stupid or show off.

That said, I have been on some sensible group rides, and have conducted more than a few. For several years CLASS conducted a tour of Norway. So I know group riding can be a fun, safe experience if the right suggestions and precautions are in place.

GROUP PSYCHOLOGY

The key to safe group riding is exercising your self-knowledge. You need a firm understanding of yourself and your capabilities. If you can't resist the urge to follow a faster rider, you'll end up in trouble. By now you should have a "formula" for how you approach a corner, which incorporates a safe entry speed, a good line, the proper gear, good throttle management, and the correct weight shift. You've practiced your technique, and you know it works. So why deviate? In a

Racers are comfortable riding within inches of each other, at triple-digit speeds. There is an element of trust. Group riding on public roads is an entirely different matter—KEEP YOUR DISTANCE! (Ian Donald Photography)

ONE OF THE PRIMARY DANGERS IN TOWN IS THE PEOPLE YOU ARE WITH.
Don't let anyone else dictate your lane position or speed, or interfere with your view of what's around you. Rely on your own good traffic sense. Stick to the plan you've made beforehand.

group, you should stick to your formula and trust your good assessment of the road ahead. After all, you are in control. If others in the group are going faster or riding in a questionable way, you should have the confidence and self-knowledge to let them go. You can always catch up later. After all, what's the big deal? It's not worth risking your life just so you can avoid a ribbing later. Ego in this instance can kill you.

My own "formula"—the sum of all the information in this book—allows me to safely visit roads I've never been on before. To me a road is a road, and I approach it in my way, even when I'm in the company of others. Of course, this isn't to say I don't take up the challenge here and there with a rider I trust, and on a road I know well. But I always ride well within my envelope.

GROUND RULES
On those occasions when you do ride with others, it's your job to assess the leader. Check out that person's corner entry and body movements. Is he or she smooth? Is it someone you feel good about riding behind? Or is the leader obviously riding on the ragged edge of control? Even when you are confident in the leader, leave a margin of error. You never know when panic will rear its

ugly head. If the leader feels pressure to keep up a certain pace and panic sets in, the whole group can be taken down. Don't let yourself be led into that trap. Just as in normal traffic, leave an adequate cushion—at least a bike length for every 10 mph.

A good leader will accommodate a range of abilities, and perhaps hang back to let the slower ones catch up. He or she is also open to suggestions. At a rest stop, you might point out that the group is losing riders, and that it would be good to slow down. Not everyone in a group will be on the same pace, and being a leader requires judgment and understanding. During the CLASS tours of Norway, I reminded everyone throughout the day to leave a margin of safety. We always provided an opportunity for the slower riders to catch up.

The leader should make the ground rules apparent at the outset. What is the route and final destination? Are there standard signals to be used to indicate gas or rest stops? Will there be a following rider to ensure that the group stays together? Everyone will benefit from that information.

GROUP RIDING THROUGH TOWN
Staying with a group through town is particularly challenging. Someone will always be lagging, and will therefore be tempted to jump a light or accelerate to catch up. You need to apply the same self-knowledge in these situations that you would on the open road. If it's a good group, with a good leader, they will provide you with an opportunity to catch up. If a leader blasts away from every light, it increases the temptation of those behind to make up ground by riding dangerously. It's better to let them go.

One of the primary dangers in town is the group of people you are with. Don't let anyone else dictate your lane position or speed, or interfere with your view of what's around you. Rely on your own good traffic sense.

Some riders recommend a "staggered" formation in traffic, which allows more riders to occupy a small space and stay together. In this formation, one rider is to the left, riding about two seconds behind the rider in front. Another rider is one second behind him, but to the right, and so on. Some large groups are able to make this work quite well on straight, open roads. However, I don't recommend this for roads that are in the least bit narrow or twisty, as it puts one rider out on the yellow line and in the path of oncoming traffic. It also reduces the view of what's ahead. As a result, I rarely do it.

Whether you ride in a normal line or a staggered formation, here's a word to the wise: Don't feel bad telling the rider behind to back off. If they are following too close, just one quick distraction can have a terrible consequence.

TOURING

For several years I conducted CLASS's group tour on the fantastic roads of Norway. However, even though we were a group, I made it known to everyone that it was not a regimented tour. There was no speed requirement. Everyone was supplied with accurate maps and required to know where we were going. The slower riders could leave a little earlier, and the racers left a little later.

I offered people the opportunity to ride with me but did not require it. I told them some of the likely stopping points during the day (for Norwegian ice cream and waffles!), and we often met there, with riders trickling in over the period of a half hour or so. It worked well, because we had established these ground rules up front, and we didn't force anyone to ride outside their particular envelopes.

PICKING UP STRANGERS

Sometimes you'll end up with other riders spontaneously, because you are overtaken or because you overtake someone yourself. When passing a slower rider, pick your point carefully. Ensure that you have a safe margin and don't surprise the person—you never know what they'll do or what the results will be.

Conversely, if a fast guy comes up on the back of you, it's often best to pull over and let him or her go by. After all, you have no way of knowing that person's capability or whether they are trustworthy. What's more, the guy can give you a real shock if you are passed in a dangerous spot—another reason I don't permit unfamiliar riders to follow too closely. I also have the ability to use a lot of engine braking, even downshifting at 12,000 rpm, and this lack of brake lights means it isn't always apparent to the person behind when I am slowing.

THIS LOOKS LIKE A SAFE PLACE TO DO A LITTLE DAYDREAMING—WRONG! *Some riders recommend a "staggered" formation. However, I don't recommend this for roads that are in the least bit narrow or twisty, as it puts one rider out on the yellow line and in the path of oncoming traffic. It also reduces the view of what's ahead. As a result, I rarely do it. (Photo courtesy Woman Rider magazine)*

INDEX

Whitehorse Press
the motorcycle information company

107 East Conway Road,
Center Conway, NH 03813-4012
www.whitehorsepress.com
CALL TOLL-FREE 1-800-531-1133

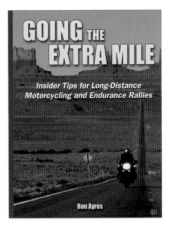

Softbound
8-1/4 x 10-1/2 inches
176 pages
approx. 200 color
photos & illustrations

ISBN: 1-884313-47-7
Order Code: MCX2
Price: $24.95

Softbound
8-1/4 x 10-1/2 inches
144 pages
b/w illus.

ISBN: 1-884313-39-6
Order Code: GEM
Price: $19.95

Motorcycling Excellence (Second Edition)
The Motorcycle Safety Foundation

Here is a book for the motorcyclist who wants to do it right—the most complete, authoritative book ever published on safe riding techniques and strategies. Statistics indicate that a substantial percentage of motorcycle accidents involve riders with limited experience and training. Prior to 1973 there were few organized programs to instruct both beginners and experienced riders in safe motorcycle operation. Since that time, over one million students have completed courses developed by the MSF. This book is the result of teaching students of all ages and experience.

Going the Extra Mile
by Ron Ayres

Jam-packed with advice from long-distance motorcycle travel veterans, and written by best-selling author Ron Ayres, this handbook can help you extend your range on a motorcycle. Written for anyone who wants to comfortably spend more time in the saddle and less time waiting at the next rest stop, this book compiles the proven techniques that can make your next long motorcycle trip fun, safe, and comfortable. Included in this extensive and thorough work is a resource directory that's worth the price of the book alone!

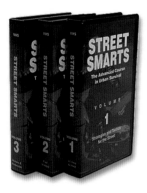

Street Smarts Videos
VHS, NTSC std., color

Street Smarts Videos are a practical course in two-wheeled street survival. With tips and tactics from experienced street riders and expert road racers, you'll learn safety techniques you can apply directly to your street riding.

Volume 1: Strategies & Tactics for the Street
STRTV $29.95
Volume 2: Lessons From the Track
SSV2. . . . . $29.95
Volume 3: Danger Zones
SSV3. . . . . $29.95
Street Smarts Video Set
SET3. . . . . $79.95

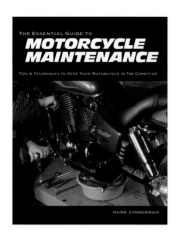

Softbound
8-1/4 x 10-1/2 inches
256 pages
color photos & illus.

ISBN: 1-884313-41-8
Order Code: EGMM
Price: $29.95

The Essential Guide to Motorcycle Maintenance
by Mark Zimmerman

This book introduces the novice motorcycle mechanic to the routine mechanical concepts that go into designing, building, and maintaining modern motorcycles. The author assumes that the reader has little or no mechanical knowledge, few tools, and will be working under the old shade tree in his back yard. The author tackles this subject with humor—making the learning process entertaining and accessible.

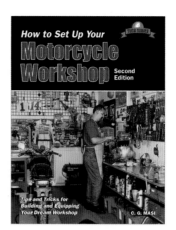

Softbound
8-1/4 x 10-1/2 inches
176 pages
b/w photos & illus.

ISBN: 1-884313-43-4
Order Code: MASI2
Price: $19.95

How To Set Up Your Motorcycle Workshop, 2nd Ed.
by C. G. Masi

From a corner of the garage set up for routine maintenance to a dream shop housing precious classic machines, this book will help you make the most of your space. Packed with easy-to-read practical advice, author Charles Masi walks the reader through designing, building, and equipping the workshop you need—whether you plan to restore, repair, and maintain your own bikes or hope to open a small commercial facility.

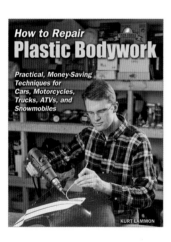

Softbound
8-1/4 x 10-1/2 inches
144 pages
color photos & illus.

ISBN: 1-884313-37-X
Order Code: PLAS
Price: $24.95

How To Repair Plastic Bodywork
by Kurt Lammon

It's a familiar story—a simple accident in the driveway results in cracked and broken bodywork that costs thousands of dollars to replace—more, sometimes, than the vehicle may be worth. Few repair shops or Do-It-Yourselfers have been interested or had the wherewithal to attempt plastic repairs, leaving no options but part replacement on an otherwise perfectly serviceable machine. In fact, insurance rates on some motorcycles and snowmobiles have skyrocketed because of the high cost of replacing broken plastic.

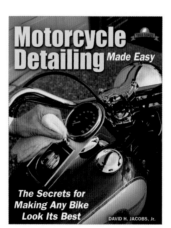

Softbound
8-1/4 x 10-1/2 inches
144 pages
b/w photos & illus.

ISBN: 1-884313-35-3
Order Code: MDME
Price: $19.95

Motorcycle Detailing Made Easy
by David H. Jacobs, Jr.

And you thought you knew how to clean your bike. Think again! Dave Jacobs will teach you things you didn't even know you didn't know. Whether you want to return your bike to showroom condition, get it ready to sell, or prepare it for a custom show, this book will help you learn what cleaning a bike is all about. Plenty of photos are included to illustrate all the procedures. Learn the tricks that will help you make your bike look great and keep it looking great.

ABOUT THE AUTHORS

When Reg Pridmore decided to put the lessons he teaches at his CLASS riding schools into book form, he turned to writer Geoff Drake to collaborate. Drake is a lifelong motorcyclist and the former editor of *Bicycling Magazine*. He has written for numerous national magazines on a variety of subjects, including *American Motorcyclist, Men's Health, Mountain Bike, Rider,* and *VeloNews,* the Journal of Competitive Cycling. He has also edited and contributed to several books. Geoff is also active in endurance sports and is an Ironman triathlete. He lives with his wife and daughter in Aptos, California.

THE PREMIER STREET RIDING SCHOOL IN THE USA

CLASS is about being a better rider. So if you're a street rider, a sport rider, or even an aspiring racer looking to get better, you've come to the right place. The school is intended for street and sport riders of varying experience and skill levels. It's for riders seeking more confidence—and for riders with too much confidence who have decided to back it up with some sound technique and track practice. For riders who know that no matter what their experience level, there's always something to learn. These days there are lots of places to go to ride the track, and only a small handful of these include proper instruction. CLASS has been the leader in teaching the finer aspects of smoothness and control of street riding for more than 20 years.

CLASS MOTORCYCLE SCHOOL
S320 E. SANTA MARIA STREET SUITE "M"
SANTA PAULA, CA 93060
(805) 933-9936

WWW.CLASSRIDES.COM